Terraform: Up and Running
Writing Infrastructure as Code

Yevgeniy Brikman

Beijing · Boston · Farnham · Sebastopol · Tokyo

Terraform: Up and Running

by Yevgeniy Brikman

Printed in the United States of America.

Published by O'Reilly Media, Inc., 1005 Gravenstein Highway North, Sebastopol, CA 95472.

O'Reilly books may be purchased for educational, business, or sales promotional use. Online editions are also available for most titles (*http://oreilly.com/safari*). For more information, contact our corporate/institutional sales department: 800-998-9938 or *corporate@oreilly.com*.

Editors: Brian Anderson and Virginia Wilson
Production Editor: Nicholas Adams
Copyeditor: James Fraleigh
Proofreader: Kim Cofer

Indexer: Ellen Troutman-Zaig
Interior Designer: David Futato
Cover Designer: Randy Comer
Illustrator: Rebecca Demarest

March 2017:   First Edition

Revision History for the First Edition
2017-03-07:   First Release

See *http://oreilly.com/catalog/errata.csp?isbn=9781491977088* for release details.

978-1-491-97708-8

[LSI]

To Mom, Dad, Lyalya, and Molly

Table of Contents

Preface

A long time ago, in a data center far, far away, an ancient group of powerful beings known as sysadmins used to deploy infrastructure manually. Every server, every database, every load balancer, and every bit of network configuration was created and managed by hand. It was a dark and fearful age: fear of downtime, fear of accidental misconfiguration, fear of slow and fragile deployments, and fear of what would happen if the sysadmins fell to the dark side (i.e., took a vacation). The good news is that thanks to the DevOps movement, there is now a better way to do things: Terraform.

Terraform (*https://www.terraform.io/*) is an open source tool created by HashiCorp that allows you to define your infrastructure as code using a simple, declarative programming language, and to deploy and manage that infrastructure across a variety of public cloud providers (e.g., Amazon Web Services, Azure, Google Cloud, DigitalOcean) and private cloud and virtualization platforms (e.g., OpenStack, VMWare) using a few commands. For example, instead of manually clicking around a web page or running dozens of commands, here is all the code it takes to configure a server on Amazon Web Services:

```
provider "aws" {
  region = "us-east-1"
}

resource "aws_instance" "example" {
  ami           = "ami-40d28157"
  instance_type = "t2.micro"
}
```

And to deploy it, you just run one command:

```
> terraform apply
```

Thanks to its simplicity and power, Terraform is rapidly emerging as a key player in the DevOps world. It allows you to replace the tedious, fragile, and manual parts of sysadmin work with a solid, automated foundation upon which you can build all your other DevOps practices (e.g., automated testing, continuous integration, continuous delivery) and tooling (e.g., Docker, Chef, Puppet).

This book is the fastest way to get up and running with Terraform.

You'll go from deploying the most basic "Hello, World" Terraform example (in fact, you just saw it!) all the way up to running a full tech stack (server cluster, load balancer, database) capable of supporting a large amount of traffic and a large team of developers—all in the span of just a few chapters. This is a hands-on tutorial that not only teaches you DevOps and infrastructure as code principles, but also walks you through dozens of code examples that you can try at home, so make sure you have your computer handy.

By the time you're done, you'll be ready to use Terraform in the real world.

Who Should Read This Book

This book is for anyone responsible for the code after it has been written. That includes Sysadmins, Operations Engineers, Release Engineers, Site Reliability Engineers, DevOps Engineers, Infrastructure Developers, Full Stack Developers, Engineering Managers, and CTOs. No matter what your title is, if you're the one managing infrastructure, deploying code, configuring servers, scaling clusters, backing up data, monitoring apps, and responding to alerts at 3 a.m., then this book is for you.

Collectively, all of these tasks are usually referred to as "operations." In the past, it was common to find developers who knew how to write code, but did not understand operations; likewise, it was common to find sysadmins who understood operations, but did not know how to write code. You could get away with that divide in the past, but in the modern world, as cloud computing and the DevOps movement become ubiquitous, just about every developer will need to learn operational skills and every sysadmin will need to learn coding skills.

This book does not assume you're already an expert coder or expert sysadmin—a basic familiarity with programming, the command line, and server-based software (e.g., websites) should suffice. Everything else you need you'll be able to pick up as you go, so that by the end of the book, you will have a solid grasp of one of the most critical aspects of modern development and operations: managing infrastructure as code.

In fact, you'll learn not only how to manage infrastructure as code using Terraform, but also how this fits into the overall DevOps world. Here are some of the questions you'll be able to answer by the end of the book:

- Why use infrastructure as code at all?
- What are the differences between configuration management, provisioning, and server templating?
- When should you use Terraform, Chef, Ansible, Puppet, Salt, CloudFormation, Docker, or Packer?
- How does Terraform work and how do you use it to manage your infrastructure?
- How do you make Terraform a part of your automated deployment process?
- How do you make Terraform a part of your automated testing process?
- What are the best practices for using Terraform as a team?

The only tools you need are a computer (Terraform runs on most operating systems), an internet connection, and the desire to learn.

Why I Wrote This Book

Terraform is a powerful tool. It works with all popular cloud providers. It uses a clean, simple language with strong support for reuse, testing, and versioning. It's open source and has a friendly, active community. But there is one area where it's lacking: age.

At the time of writing, Terraform is barely two years old. As a result, it's hard to find books, blog posts, or experts to help you master the tool. If you try to learn Terraform from the official documentation, you'll find that it does a good job of introducing the basic syntax and features, but it includes almost no information on idiomatic patterns, best practices, testing, reusability, or team workflows. It's like trying to become fluent in French by studying only the vocabulary and not any of the grammar or idioms.

The reason I wrote this book is to help developers become fluent in Terraform. I've been using Terraform for more than half of its life, much of it in a professional context at my company Gruntwork (*http://www.gruntwork.io*), and I've spent many of those months figuring out what works and what doesn't primarily through trial and error. My goal is to share what I've learned so you can avoid that lengthy process and become fluent in a matter of hours.

Of course, you can't become fluent just by reading. To become fluent in French, you'll have to spend time talking with native French speakers, watching French TV shows, and listening to French music. To become fluent in Terraform, you'll have to write real Terraform code, use it to manage real software, and deploy that software on real servers. Therefore, be ready to read, write, and execute a lot of code.

What You Will Find in This Book

Here's an outline of what the book covers:

Chapter 1, Why Terraform
> How DevOps is transforming the way we run software; an overview of infrastructure as code tools, including configuration management, provisioning, and server templating; the benefits of infrastructure as code; a comparison of Terraform, Chef, Puppet, Ansible, SaltStack, OpenStack Heat, and CloudFormation.

Chapter 2, Getting Started with Terraform
> Installing Terraform; an overview of Terraform syntax; an overview of the Terraform CLI tool; how to deploy a single server; how to deploy a web server; how to deploy a cluster of web servers; how to deploy a load balancer; how to clean up resources you've created.

Chapter 3, How to Manage Terraform State
> What is Terraform state; how to store state so multiple team members can access it; how to lock state files to prevent race conditions; how to isolate state files to limit the damage from errors; a best-practices file and folder layout for Terraform projects; how to use read-only state.

Chapter 4, How to Create Reusable Infrastructure with Terraform Modules
> What are modules; how to create a basic module; how to make a module configurable; versioned modules; module tips and tricks; using modules to define reusable, configurable pieces of infrastructure.

Chapter 5, Terraform Tips and Tricks: Loops, If-Statements, Deployment, and Gotchas
> Advanced Terraform syntax; loops; if-statements; if-else statements; interpolation functions; zero-downtime deployment; common Terraform gotchas and pitfalls.

Chapter 6, How to Use Terraform as a Team
> Version control; the golden rule of Terraform; coding guidelines; Terraform style; automated testing for Terraform; documentation; a workflow for teams; automation with Terraform.

Feel free to read the book from start to finish or jump around to the chapters that interest you the most. At the end of the book, in Appendix A, you'll find a list of recommended reading where you can learn more about Terraform, operations, infrastructure as code, and DevOps.

What You Won't Find in This Book

This book is not meant to be an exhaustive reference manual for Terraform. I do not cover all the cloud providers, or all of the resources supported by each cloud provider, or every available Terraform command. For these nitty-gritty details, I refer you instead to the Terraform documentation (*https://www.terraform.io/docs/index.html*).

The documentation contains many useful answers, but if you're new to Terraform, infrastructure as code, or operations, you won't even know what questions to ask. Therefore, this book is focused on what the documentation does *not* cover: namely, how to go beyond introductory examples and use Terraform in a real-world setting. My goal is to get you up and running quickly by discussing why you may want to use Terraform in the first place, how to fit it into your workflow, and what practices and patterns tend to work best.

To demonstrate these patterns, I've included a number of code examples. I've tried to make it as easy as possible for you to try these examples at home by minimizing dependencies on any third parties. This is why almost all the examples use just a single cloud provider, Amazon Web Services (AWS), so you only have to sign up for a single third-party service (also, AWS offers a generous free tier, so running the example code shouldn't cost you anything). This is why the book and the example code do not cover or require HashiCorp's paid services, Terraform Pro and Terraform Enterprise. And this is why I've released all the code examples as open source.

Open Source Code Examples

All of the code samples in the book can be found at the following URL:

https://github.com/brikis98/terraform-up-and-running-code

You may want to check out this repo before you start reading so you can follow along with all the examples on your own computer:

```
git clone https://github.com/brikis98/terraform-up-and-running-code.git
```

The code examples in that repo are broken down chapter by chapter. It's worth noting that most of the examples show you what the code looks like at the *end* of a chapter. If you want to maximize your learning, you're better off writing the code yourself, from scratch.

You'll start coding in Chapter 2, where you'll learn how to use Terraform to deploy a basic cluster of web servers from scratch. After that, follow the instructions in each subsequent chapter on how to evolve and improve this web server cluster example. Make the changes as instructed, try to write all the code yourself, and only use the sample code in the GitHub repo as a way to check your work or get yourself unstuck.

A Note About Versions

All of the examples in this book were tested against Terraform 0.8.x, which was the most recent major release at the time of writing. Since Terraform is a relatively new tool and has not hit version 1.0.0 yet, it is possible that future releases will contain backward incompatible changes, and it is likely that some of the best practices will change and evolve over time.

I'll try to release updates as often as I can, but the Terraform project moves fast, so you'll have to do some work to keep up with it on your own. For the latest news, blog posts, and talks on Terraform and DevOps, be sure to check out this book's website and subscribe to the newsletter!

Using the Code Examples

This book is here to help you get your job done and you are welcome to use the sample code in your programs and documentation. You do not need to contact O'Reilly for permission unless you're reproducing a significant portion of the code. For example, writing a program that uses several chunks of code from this book does not require permission. Selling or distributing a CD-ROM of examples from O'Reilly books does require permission. Answering a question by citing this book and quoting example code does not require permission. Incorporating a significant amount of example code from this book into your product's documentation does require permission.

Attribution is appreciated, but not required. An attribution usually includes the title, author, publisher, and ISBN. For example: "*Terraform: Up and Running* by Yevgeniy Brikman (O'Reilly). Copyright 2017 Yevgeniy Brikman, 978-1-491-97708-8."

If you feel your use of code examples falls outside fair use or the permission given above, feel free to contact O'Reilly Media at *permissions@oreilly.com*.

Conventions Used in This Book

The following typographical conventions are used in this book:

Italic
  Indicates new terms, URLs, email addresses, filenames, and file extensions.

`Constant width`
  Used for program listings, as well as within paragraphs to refer to program elements such as variable or function names, databases, data types, environment variables, statements, and keywords.

Constant width bold

Shows commands or other text that should be typed literally by the user.

Constant width italic

Shows text that should be replaced with user-supplied values or by values determined by context.

 This element signifies a tip or suggestion.

 This element signifies a general note.

 This element indicates a warning or caution.

O'Reilly Safari

 *Safari* (formerly Safari Books Online) is a membership-based training and reference platform for enterprise, government, educators, and individuals.

Members have access to thousands of books, training videos, Learning Paths, interactive tutorials, and curated playlists from over 250 publishers, including O'Reilly Media, Harvard Business Review, Prentice Hall Professional, Addison-Wesley Professional, Microsoft Press, Sams, Que, Peachpit Press, Adobe, Focal Press, Cisco Press, John Wiley & Sons, Syngress, Morgan Kaufmann, IBM Redbooks, Packt, Adobe Press, FT Press, Apress, Manning, New Riders, McGraw-Hill, Jones & Bartlett, and Course Technology, among others.

For more information, please visit *http://oreilly.com/safari*.

How to Contact O'Reilly Media

Please address comments and questions concerning this book to the publisher:

O'Reilly Media, Inc.
1005 Gravenstein Highway North
Sebastopol, CA 95472
800-998-9938 (in the United States or Canada)
707-829-0515 (international or local)
707-829-0104 (fax)

We have a web page for this book, where we list errata, examples, and any additional information. You can access this page at *http://bit.ly/terraform-up-and-running*.

To comment or ask technical questions about this book, send email to *bookquestions@oreilly.com*.

For more information about our books, courses, conferences, and news, see our website at *http://www.oreilly.com*.

Find us on Facebook: *http://facebook.com/oreilly*

Follow us on Twitter: *http://twitter.com/oreillymedia*

Watch us on YouTube: *http://www.youtube.com/oreillymedia*

Acknowledgments

Josh Padnick

This book would not have been possible without you. You were the one who introduced me to Terraform in the first place, taught me all the basics, and helped me figure out all the advanced parts. Thank you for supporting me while I took our collective learnings and turned them into a book. Thank you for being an awesome cofounder and making it possible to run a startup while still living a fun life. And thank you most of all for being a good friend and a good person.

O'Reilly Media

Thank you for publishing another one of my books. Reading and writing have profoundly transformed my life and I'm proud to have your help in sharing some of my writing with others. A special thanks to Brian Anderson for helping me get this book out in record time.

Gruntwork customers

Thank you for taking a chance on a small, unknown company, and volunteering to be guinea pigs for our Terraform experiments. Gruntwork's mission is to make it an order of magnitude easier to understand, develop, and deploy software. We haven't always succeeded at that mission (I've captured many of our mistakes in this book!), so I'm grateful for your patience and willingness to be part of our audacious attempt to improve the world of software.

HashiCorp
Thank you for building an amazing collection of DevOps tools, including Terraform, Packer, Consul, and Vault. You've improved the world of DevOps and with it, the lives of millions of software developers.

Kief Morris, Seth Vargo, Mattias Gees
Thank you for reading an early version of this book and providing lots of detailed, constructive feedback. Your suggestions have made this book significantly better.

Mom, Dad, Larisa, Molly
I accidentally wrote another book. That probably means I didn't spend as much time with you as I wanted. Thank you for putting up with me anyway. I love you.

## CHAPTER 1

Why Terraform

Software isn't done when the code is working on your computer. It's not done when the tests pass. And it's not done when someone gives you a "ship it" on a code review. Software isn't done until you *deliver* it to the user.

Software delivery consists of all the work you need to do to make the code available to a customer, such as running that code on production servers, making the code resilient to outages and traffic spikes, and protecting the code from attackers. Before you dive into the details of Terraform, it's worth taking a step back to see where Terraform fits into the bigger picture of software delivery.

In this chapter, I'll dive into the following topics:

- The rise of DevOps
- What is infrastructure as code?
- Benefits of infrastructure as code
- How Terraform works
- How Terraform compares to other infrastructure as code tools

The Rise of DevOps

In the not-so-distant past, if you wanted to build a software company, you also had to manage a lot of hardware. You would set up cabinets and racks, load them up with servers, hook up wiring, install cooling, build redundant power systems, and so on. It made sense to have one team, typically called Operations ("Ops"), dedicated to managing this hardware, and a separate team, typically called Developers ("Devs"), dedicated to writing the software.

The typical Dev team would build an application and "toss it over the wall" to the Ops team. It was then up to Ops to figure out how to deploy and run that application. Most of this was done manually. In part, that was unavoidable, because much of the work had to do with physically hooking up hardware (e.g., racking servers, hooking up network cables). But even the work Ops did in software, such as installing the application and its dependencies, was often done by manually executing commands on a server.

This works well for a while, but as the company grows, you eventually run into problems. It typically plays out like this: since releases are done manually, as the number of servers increases, releases become slow, painful, and unpredictable. The Ops team occasionally makes mistakes, so you end up with *snowflake servers*, where each one has a subtly different configuration from all the others (a problem known as *configuration drift*). As a result, the number of bugs increases. Developers shrug and say "It works on my machine!" Outages and downtime become more frequent.

The Ops team, tired from their pagers going off at 3 a.m. after every release, reduce the release cadence to once per week. Then to once per month. Then once every six months. Weeks before the biannual release, teams start trying to merge all their projects together, leading to a huge mess of merge conflicts. No one can stabilize the release branch. Teams start blaming each other. Silos form. The company grinds to a halt.

Nowadays, a profound shift is taking place. Instead of managing their own data centers, many companies are moving to the cloud, taking advantage of services such as Amazon Web Services, Azure, and Google Cloud. Instead of investing heavily in hardware, many Ops teams are spending all their time working on software, using tools such as Chef, Puppet, Terraform, and Docker. Instead of racking servers and plugging in network cables, many sysadmins are writing code.

As a result, both Dev and Ops spend most of their time working on software, and the distinction between the two teams is blurring. It may still make sense to have a separate Dev team responsible for the application code and an Ops team responsible for the operational code, but it's clear that Dev and Ops need to work more closely together. This is where the *DevOps movement* comes from.

DevOps isn't the name of a team or a job title or a particular technology. Instead, it's a set of processes, ideas, and techniques. Everyone has a slightly different definition of DevOps, but for this book, I'm going to go with the following:

> *The goal of DevOps is to make software delivery vastly more efficient.*

Instead of multiday merge nightmares, you integrate code continuously and always keep it in a deployable state. Instead of deploying code once per month, you can deploy code dozens of times per day, or even after every single commit. And instead of constant outages and downtime, you build resilient, self-healing systems, and use monitoring and alerting to catch problems that can't be resolved automatically.

The results from companies that have undergone DevOps transformations are astounding. For example, Nordstrom found that after applying DevOps practices to its organization, it was able to double the number of features it delivered per month, reduce defects by 50%, reduce *lead times* (the time from coming up with an idea to running code in production) by 60%, and reduce the number of production incidents by 60% to 90%. After HP's LaserJet Firmware division began using DevOps practices, the amount of time its developers spent on developing new features went from 5% to 40% and overall development costs were reduced by 40%. Etsy used DevOps practices to go from stressful, infrequent deployments that caused numerous outages to deploying 25 to 50 times per day, with far fewer outages.[1]

There are four core values in the DevOps movement: Culture, Automation, Measurement, and Sharing (sometimes abbreviated as the acronym CAMS (*http://devopsdictionary.com/wiki/CAMS*)). This book is not meant as a comprehensive overview of DevOps (check out Appendix A for recommended reading), so I will just focus on one of these values: automation.

The goal is to automate as much of the software delivery process as possible. That means that you manage your infrastructure not by clicking around a web page or manually executing shell commands, but through code. This is a concept that is typically called infrastructure as code.

What Is Infrastructure as Code?

The idea behind *infrastructure as code (IAC)* is that you write and execute code to define, deploy, and update your infrastructure. This represents an important shift in mindset where you treat all aspects of operations as software—even those aspects that represent hardware (e.g., setting up physical servers). In fact, a key insight of DevOps is that you can manage almost *everything* in code, including servers, databases, networks, log files, application configuration, documentation, automated tests, deployment processes, and so on.

There are four broad categories of IAC tools:

- Ad hoc scripts
- Configuration management tools

---

1 From *The DevOps Handbook: How to Create World-Class Agility, Reliability, & Security in Technology Organizations* (IT Revolution Press) by Gene Kim, Jez Humble, Patrick Debois, and John Willis (*http://itrevolution.com/devops-handbook*).

- Server templating tools
- Server provisioning tools

Let's look at these one at a time.

Ad Hoc Scripts

The most straightforward approach to automating anything is to write an *ad hoc script*. You take whatever task you were doing manually, break it down into discrete steps, use your favorite scripting language (e.g., Bash, Ruby, Python) to define each of those steps in code, and execute that script on your server, as shown in Figure 1-1.

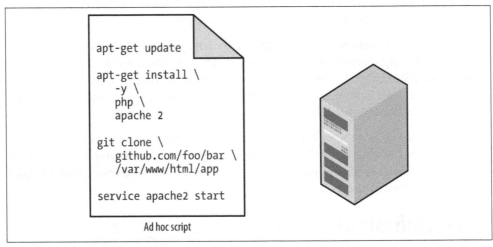

Figure 1-1. Running an ad hoc script on your server

For example, here is a Bash script called *setup-webserver.sh* that configures a web server by installing dependencies, checking out some code from a Git repo, and firing up the Apache web server:

```
# Update the apt-get cache
sudo apt-get update

# Install PHP
sudo apt-get install -y php

# Install Apache
sudo apt-get install -y apache2

# Copy the code from the repository
sudo git clone https://github.com/brikis98/php-app.git /var/www/html/app

# Start Apache
sudo service apache2 start
```

The great thing about ad hoc scripts is that you can use popular, general-purpose programming languages and you can write the code however you want. The terrible thing about ad hoc scripts is that you can use popular, general-purpose programming languages and you can write the code however you want.

Whereas tools that are purpose-built for IAC provide concise APIs for accomplishing complicated tasks, if you're using a general-purpose programming language, you have to write completely custom code for every task. Moreover, tools designed for IAC usually enforce a particular structure for your code, whereas with a general-purpose programming language, each developer will use his or her own style and do something different. Neither of these problems is a big deal for an eight-line script that installs Apache, but it gets messy if you try to use ad hoc scripts to manage dozens of servers, databases, load balancers, network configurations, and so on.

If you've ever had to maintain someone else's repository of ad hoc scripts, you know that it almost always devolves into a mess of unmaintainable spaghetti code. Ad hoc scripts are great for small, one-off tasks, but if you're going to be managing all of your infrastructure as code, then you should use an IAC tool that is purpose-built for the job.

Configuration Management Tools

Chef, Puppet, Ansible, and SaltStack are all *configuration management tools*, which means they are designed to install and manage software on existing servers. For example, here is an *Ansible Role* called *web-server.yml* that configures the same Apache web server as the *setup-webserver.sh* script:

```
- name: Update the apt-get cache
  apt:
    update_cache: yes

- name: Install PHP
  apt:
    name: php

- name: Install Apache
  apt:
    name: apache2

- name: Copy the code from the repository
  git: repo=https://github.com/brikis98/php-app.git dest=/var/www/html/app

- name: Start Apache
  service: name=apache2 state=started enabled=yes
```

The code looks similar to the Bash script, but using a tool like Ansible offers a number of advantages:

Coding conventions

Ansible enforces a consistent, predictable structure, including documentation, file layout, clearly named parameters, secrets management, and so on. While every developer organizes his or her ad hoc scripts in a different way, most configuration management tools come with a set of conventions that makes it easier to navigate the code.

Idempotence

Writing an ad hoc script that works once isn't too difficult; writing an ad hoc script that works correctly even if you run it over and over again is a lot harder. Every time you go to create a folder in your script, you need to remember to check if that folder already exists; every time you add a line of configuration to a file, you need to check that line doesn't already exist; every time you want to run an app, you need to check that the app isn't already running.

Code that works correctly no matter how many times you run it is called *idempotent code*. To make the Bash script from the previous section idempotent, you'd have to add many lines of code, including lots of if-statements. Most Ansible functions, on the other hand, are idempotent by default. For example, the *webserver.yml* Ansible role will only install Apache if it isn't installed already and will only try to start the Apache web server if it isn't running already.

Distribution

Ad hoc scripts are designed to run on a single, local machine. Ansible and other configuration management tools are designed specifically for managing large numbers of remote servers, as shown in Figure 1-2.

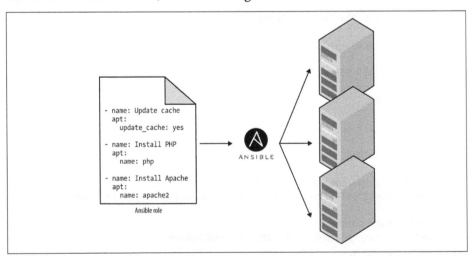

Figure 1-2. A configuration management tool like Ansible can execute your code across a large number of servers

For example, to apply the *web-server.yml* role to five servers, you first create a file called *hosts* that contains the IP addresses of those servers:

```
[webservers]
11.11.11.11
11.11.11.12
11.11.11.13
11.11.11.14
11.11.11.15
```

Next, you define the following *Ansible Playbook*:

```
- hosts: webservers
  roles:
  - webserver
```

Finally, you execute the playbook as follows:

```
ansible-playbook playbook.yml
```

This will tell Ansible to configure all five servers in parallel. Alternatively, by setting a single parameter called `serial` in the playbook, you can do a rolling deployment, which updates the servers in batches. For example, setting `serial` to 2 will tell Ansible to update two of the servers at a time, until all five are done. Duplicating any of this logic in an ad hoc script will take dozens or even hundreds of lines of code.

Server Templating Tools

An alternative to configuration management that has been growing in popularity recently are *server templating tools* such as Docker, Packer, and Vagrant. Instead of launching a bunch of servers and configuring them by running the same code on each one, the idea behind server templating tools is to create an *image* of a server that captures a fully self-contained "snapshot" of the operating system, the software, the files, and all other relevant details. You can then use some other IAC tool to install that image on all of your servers, as shown in Figure 1-3.

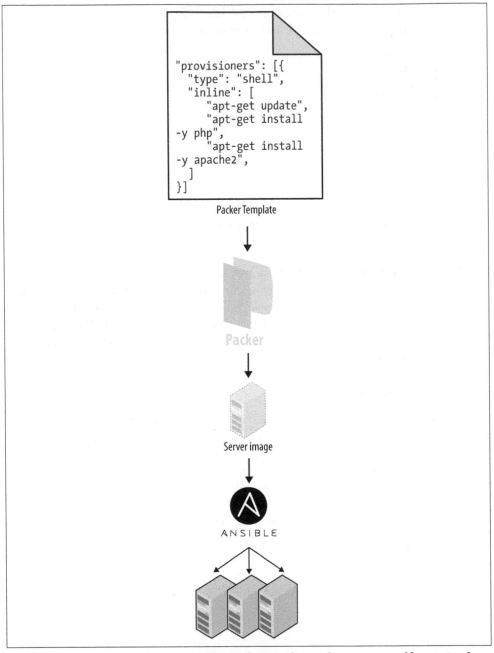

Figure 1-3. A server templating tool like Packer can be used to create a self-contained image of a server. You can then use other tools, such as Ansible, to install that image across all of your servers.

As shown in Figure 1-4, there are two broad categories of tools for working with images:

Virtual Machines

A *virtual machine (VM)* emulates an entire computer system, including the hardware. You run a *hypervisor*, such as VMWare, VirtualBox, or Parallels, to virtualize (i.e., simulate) the underlying CPU, memory, hard drive, and networking. The benefit of this is that any *VM Image* you run on top of the hypervisor can only see the virtualized hardware, so it's fully isolated from the host machine and any other VM Images, and will run exactly the same way in all environments (e.g., your computer, a QA server, a production server, etc). The drawback is that virtualizing all this hardware and running a totally separate operating system for each VM incurs a lot of overhead in terms of CPU usage, memory usage, and startup time. You can define VM Images as code using tools such as Packer and Vagrant.

Containers

A *container* emulates the user space of an operating system.[2] You run a *container engine*, such as Docker or CoreOS rkt, to create isolated processes, memory, mount points, and networking. The benefit of this is that any container you run on top of the container engine can only see its own user space, so it's isolated from the host machine and other containers, and will run exactly the same way in all environments (e.g., your computer, a QA server, a production server, etc.). The drawback is that all the containers running on a single server share that server's operating system kernel and hardware, so the isolation is not as secure as with VMs.[3] However, because the kernel and hardware are shared, your containers can boot up in milliseconds and have virtually no CPU or memory overhead. You can define Container Images as code using tools such as Docker and CoreOs rkt.

---

2 On most modern operating systems, code runs in one of two "spaces": *kernel space* and *user space*. Code running in kernel space has direct, unrestricted access to all of the hardware. There are no security restrictions (i.e., you can execute any CPU instruction, access any part of the hard drive, write to any address in memory) or safety restrictions (e.g., a crash in kernel space will typically crash the entire computer), so kernel space is generally reserved for the lowest-level, most trusted functions of the operating system (typically called the *kernel*). Code running in user space does not have any direct access to the hardware and must use APIs exposed by the operating system kernel instead. These APIs can enforce security restrictions (e.g., user permissions) and safety (e.g., a crash in a user space app typically only affects that app), so just about all application code runs in user space.

3 As a general rule, containers provide isolation that's good enough to run your own code, but if you need to run third-party code (e.g., you're building your own cloud provider) that may actively be performing malicious actions, you'll want the increased isolation guarantees of a VM.

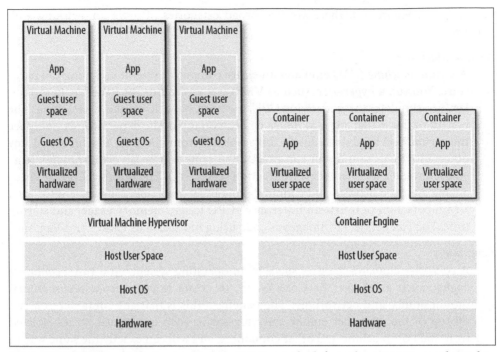

Figure 1-4. The two main types of images: VMs, on the left, and containers, on the right. VMs virtualize the hardware, whereas containers only virtualize user space.

For example, here is a Packer template called *web-server.json* that creates an *Amazon Machine Image* (AMI), which is a VM Image you can run on Amazon Web Services (AWS):

```
{
  "builders": [{
    "ami_name": "packer-example",
    "instance_type": "t2.micro",
    "region": "us-east-1",
    "type": "amazon-ebs",
    "source_ami": "ami-40d28157",
    "ssh_username": "ubuntu"
  }],
  "provisioners": [{
    "type": "shell",
    "inline": [
      "sudo apt-get update",
      "sudo apt-get install -y php",
      "sudo apt-get install -y apache2",
      "sudo git clone https://github.com/brikis98/php-app.git /var/www/html/app"
    ]
  }]
}
```

This Packer template configures the same Apache web server you saw in *setup-webserver.sh* using the same Bash code.[4] The only difference between the preceding code and previous examples is that this Packer template does not start the Apache web server (e.g., by calling `sudo service apache2 start`). That's because server templates are typically used to install software in images, but it's only when you run the image (e.g., by deploying it on a server) that you should actually run that software.

You can build an AMI from this template by running `packer build web server.json`, and once the build completes, you can install that AMI on all of your AWS servers, configure each server to run Apache when the server is booting (you'll see an example of this in the next section), and they will all run exactly the same way.

Note that the different server templating tools have slightly different purposes. Packer is typically used to create images that you run directly on top of production servers, such as an AMI that you run in your production AWS account. Vagrant is typically used to create images that you run on your development computers, such as a VirtualBox image that you run on your Mac or Windows laptop. Docker is typically used to create images of individual applications. You can run the Docker images on production or development computers, so long as some other tool has configured that computer with the Docker Engine. For example, a common pattern is to use Packer to create an AMI that has the Docker Engine installed, deploy that AMI on a cluster of servers in your AWS account, and then deploy individual Docker containers across that cluster to run your applications.

Server templating is a key component of the shift to *immutable infrastructure*. This idea is inspired by functional programming, where variables are immutable, so once you've set a variable to a value, you can never change that variable again. If you need to update something, you create a new variable. Since variables never change, it's a lot easier to reason about your code.

The idea behind immutable infrastructure is similar: once you've deployed a server, you never make changes to it again. If you need to update something (e.g., deploy a new version of your code), you create a new image from your server template and you deploy it on a new server. Since servers never change, it's a lot easier to reason about what's deployed.

Server Provisioning Tools

Whereas configuration management and server templating tools define the code that runs on each server, *server provisioning tools* such as Terraform, CloudFormation, and

---

4 As an alternative to Bash, Packer also allows you to configure your images using configuration management tools such as Ansible or Chef.

OpenStack Heat are responsible for creating the servers themselves. In fact, you can use provisioning tools to not only create servers, but also databases, caches, load balancers, queues, monitoring, subnet configurations, firewall settings, routing rules, SSL certificates, and almost every other aspect of your infrastructure, as shown in Figure 1-5.

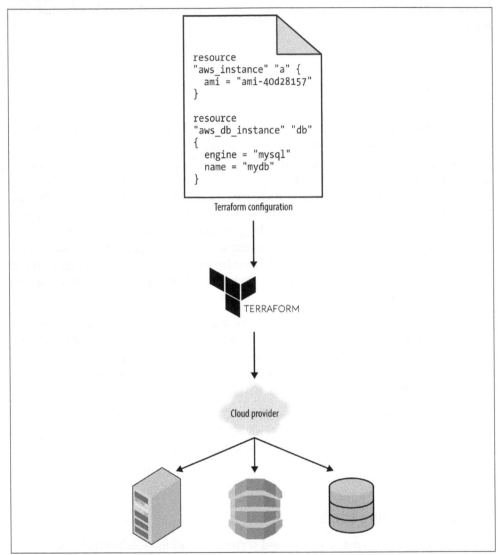

Figure 1-5. Server provisioning tools can be used with your cloud provider to create servers, databases, load balancers, and all other parts of your infrastructure.

For example, the following code deploys a web server using Terraform:

```
resource "aws_instance" "app" {
  instance_type     = "t2.micro"
  availability_zone = "us-east-1a"
  ami               = "ami-40d28157"

  user_data = <<-EOF
              #!/bin/bash
              sudo service apache2 start
              EOF
}
```

Don't worry if some of the syntax isn't familiar to you yet. For now, just focus on two parameters:

ami

> This parameter specifies the ID of an AMI to deploy on the server. You could set this parameter to the ID of an AMI built from the *web-server.json* Packer template in the previous section, which has PHP, Apache, and the application source code.

user_data

> This is a Bash script that executes when the web server is booting. The preceding code uses this script to boot up Apache.

In other words, this code shows you server provisioning and server templating working together, which is a common pattern in immutable infrastructure.

Benefits of Infrastructure as Code

Now that you've seen all the different flavors of infrastructure as code, a good question to ask is, why bother? Why learn a bunch of new languages and tools and encumber yourself with more code to manage?

The answer is that code is powerful. In exchange for the up-front investment of converting your manual practices to code, you get dramatic improvements in your ability to deliver software. According to the 2016 State of DevOps Report (*https://puppet.com/resources/white-paper/2016-state-of-devops-report*), organizations that use DevOps practices, such as IAC, deploy 200 times more frequently, recover from failures 24 times faster, and have lead times that are 2,555 times lower.

When your infrastructure is defined as code, you are able to use a wide variety of software engineering practices to dramatically improve your software delivery process, including:

Self-service

Most teams that deploy code manually have a small number of sysadmins (often, just one) who are the only ones who know all the magic incantations to make the deployment work and are the only ones with access to production. This becomes a major bottleneck as the company grows. If your infrastructure is defined in code, then the entire deployment process can be automated, and developers can kick off their own deployments whenever necessary.

Speed and safety

If the deployment process is automated, it'll be significantly faster, since a computer can carry out the deployment steps far faster than a person; and safer, since an automated process will be more consistent, more repeatable, and not prone to manual error.

Documentation

Instead of the state of your infrastructure being locked away in a single sysadmin's head, you can represent the state of your infrastructure in source files that anyone can read. In other words, IAC acts as documentation, allowing everyone in the organization to understand how things work, even if the sysadmin goes on vacation.

Version control

You can store your IAC source files in version control, which means the entire history of your infrastructure is now captured in the commit log. This becomes a powerful tool for debugging issues, as any time a problem pops up, your first step will be to check the commit log and find out what changed in your infrastructure, and your second step may be to resolve the problem by simply reverting back to a previous, known-good version of your IAC code.

Validation

If the state of your infrastructure is defined in code, then for every single change, you can perform a code review, run a suite of automated tests, and pass the code through static analysis tools, all practices that are known to significantly reduce the chance of defects.

Reuse

You can package your infrastructure into reusable modules, so that instead of doing every deployment for every product in every environment from scratch, you can build on top of known, documented, battle-tested pieces.[5]

---

5 Check out the Gruntwork Infrastructure Packages (*http://bit.ly/2lQt2UP*) for an example.

Happiness

There is one other very important, and often overlooked, reason for why you should use IAC: happiness. Deploying code and managing infrastructure manually is repetitive and tedious. Developers and sysadmins resent this type of work, as it involves no creativity, no challenge, and no recognition. You could deploy code perfectly for months, and no one will take notice—until that one day when you mess it up. That creates a stressful and unpleasant environment. IAC offers a better alternative that allows computers to do what they do best (automation) and developers to do what they do best (coding).

Now that you have a sense of why IAC is important, the next question is whether Terraform is the right IAC tool for you. To answer that, I'm first going to do a very quick primer on how Terraform works, and then I'll compare it to the other popular IAC options out there, such as Chef, Puppet, and Ansible.

How Terraform Works

Here is a high-level and somewhat simplified view of how Terraform works. Terraform is an open source tool created by HashiCorp and written in the Go programming language. The Go code compiles down into a single binary (or rather, one binary for each of the supported operating systems) called, not surprisingly, terraform.

You can use this binary to deploy infrastructure from your laptop or a build server or just about any other computer, and you don't need to run any extra infrastructure to make that happen. That's because under the hood, the terraform binary makes API calls on your behalf to one or more *providers*, such as Amazon Web Services (AWS), Azure, Google Cloud, DigitalOcean, OpenStack, etc. That means Terraform gets to leverage the infrastructure those providers are already running for their API servers, as well as the authentication mechanisms you're already using with those providers (e.g., the API keys you already have for AWS).

How does Terraform know what API calls to make? The answer is that you create *Terraform configurations*, which are text files that specify what infrastructure you wish to create. These configurations are the "code" in "infrastructure as code." Here's an example Terraform configuration:

```
resource "aws_instance" "example" {
  ami           = "ami-40d28157"
  instance_type = "t2.micro"
}

resource "dnsimple_record" "example" {
  domain = "example.com"
  name   = "test"
  value  = "${aws_instance.example.public_ip}"
```

```
type    = "A"
}
```

Even if you've never seen Terraform code before, you shouldn't have too much trouble reading it. This snippet tells Terraform to make API calls to AWS to deploy a server and then make API calls to DNSSimple to create a DNS entry pointing to the AWS server's IP address. In just a single, simple syntax (which you'll learn in Chapter 2), Terraform allows you to deploy interconnected resources across multiple cloud providers.

You can define your entire infrastructure—servers, databases, load balancers, network topology, and so on—in Terraform configuration files and commit those files to version control. You then run certain Terraform commands, such as `terraform apply`, to deploy that infrastructure. The `terraform` binary parses your code, translates it into a series of API calls to the cloud providers specified in the code, and makes those API calls as efficiently as possible on your behalf, as shown in Figure 1-6.

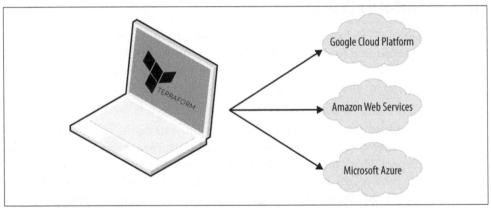

Figure 1-6. Terraform is a binary that translates the contents of your configurations into API calls to cloud providers

When someone on your team needs to make changes to the infrastructure, instead of updating the infrastructure manually and directly on the servers, they make their changes in the Terraform configuration files, validate those changes through automated tests and code reviews, commit the updated code to version control, and then run the `terraform apply` command to have Terraform make the necessary API calls to deploy the changes.

Transparent Portability Between Cloud Providers

Since Terraform supports many different cloud providers, a common question that comes up is whether it supports *transparent portability* between them. For example, if you used Terraform to define a bunch of servers, databases, load balancers, and other infrastructure in AWS, could you tell Terraform to deploy exactly the same infrastructure in another cloud provider, such as Azure or Google Cloud, in just a few clicks?

This question turns out to be a bit of a red herring. The reality is that you can't deploy "exactly the same infrastructure" in a different cloud provider because the cloud providers don't offer the same types of infrastructure! The servers, load balancers, and databases offered by AWS are very different than those in Azure and Google Cloud in terms of features, configuration, management, security, scalability, availability, observability, and so on. There is no way to "transparently" paper over these differences, especially as functionality in one cloud provider often doesn't exist at all in the others.

Terraform's approach is to allow you to write code that is specific to each provider, taking advantage of that provider's unique functionality, but to use the same language, toolset, and infrastructure as code practices under the hood for all providers.

How Terraform Compares to Other Infrastructure as Code Tools

Infrastructure as code is wonderful, but the process of picking an IAC tool is not. Many of the IAC tools overlap in what they do. Many of them are open source. Many of them offer commercial support. Unless you've used each one yourself, it's not clear what criteria you should use to pick one or the other.

What makes this even harder is that most of the comparisons you find between these tools do little more than list the general properties of each one and make it sound like you could be equally successful with any of them. And while that's technically true, it's not helpful. It's a bit like telling a programming newbie that you could be equally successful building a website with PHP, C, or assembly—a statement that's technically true, but one that omits a huge amount of information that is essential for making a good decision.

In the following sections, I'm going to do a detailed comparison between the most popular configuration management and provisioning tools: Terraform, Chef, Puppet, Ansible, SaltStack, CloudFormation, and OpenStack Heat. My goal is to help you decide if Terraform is a good choice by explaining why my company, Gruntwork (*http://www.gruntwork.io*), picked Terraform as our IAC tool of choice and, in some sense, why I wrote this book.[6] As with all technology decisions, it's a question of trade-offs and priorities, and while your particular priorities may be different than mine, I hope that sharing this thought process will help you make your own decision.

Here are the main trade-offs to consider:

- Configuration management versus provisioning
- Mutable infrastructure versus immutable infrastructure
- Procedural language versus declarative language
- Master versus masterless
- Agent versus agentless
- Large community versus small community
- Mature versus cutting-edge

Configuration Management Versus Provisioning

As you saw earlier, Chef, Puppet, Ansible, and SaltStack are all configuration management tools, whereas CloudFormation, Terraform, and OpenStack Heat are all provisioning tools. Although the distinction is not entirely clear cut, as configuration management tools can typically do some degree of provisioning (e.g., you can deploy a server with Ansible) and provisioning tools can typically do some degree of configuration (e.g., you can run configuration scripts on each server you provision with Terraform), you typically want to pick the tool that's the best fit for your use case.[7]

In particular, if you use server templating tools such as Docker or Packer, the vast majority of your configuration management needs are already taken care of. Once you have an image created from a Dockerfile or Packer template, all that's left to do is provision the infrastructure for running those images. And when it comes to provisioning, a server provisioning tool is going to be your best choice.

That said, if you're not using server templating tools, a good alternative is to use a configuration management and provisioning tool together. For example, you might use Terraform to provision your servers and run Chef to configure each one.

---

6 Docker and Packer are not part of the comparison because they can be used with any of the configuration management or provisioning tools.

7 The distinction between configuration management and provisioning has become even less clear cut in recent months, as some of the major configuration management tools have started to add better support for provisioning, such as Chef Provisioning (*https://docs.chef.io/provisioning.html*) and the Puppet AWS Module (*https://github.com/puppetlabs/puppetlabs-aws*).

Mutable Infrastructure Versus Immutable Infrastructure

Configuration management tools such as Chef, Puppet, Ansible, and SaltStack typically default to a mutable infrastructure paradigm. For example, if you tell Chef to install a new version of OpenSSL, it'll run the software update on your existing servers and the changes will happen in place. Over time, as you apply more and more updates, each server builds up a unique history of changes. As a result, each server becomes slightly different than all the others, leading to subtle configuration bugs that are difficult to diagnose and reproduce (this is the same configuration drift problem that happens when you manage servers manually, although it's much less problematic when using a configuration management tool). Even with automated tests these bugs are hard to catch, as a configuration management change may work just fine on a test server, but that same change may behave differently on a production server because the production server has accumulated months of changes that aren't reflected in the test environment.

If you're using a provisioning tool such as Terraform to deploy machine images created by Docker or Packer, then most "changes" are actually deployments of a completely new server. For example, to deploy a new version of OpenSSL, you would use Packer to create a new image with the new version of OpenSSL, deploy that image across a set of new servers, and then undeploy the old servers. Since every deployment uses immutable images on fresh servers, this approach reduces the likelihood of configuration drift bugs, makes it easier to know exactly what software is running on each server, and allows you to easily deploy any previous version of the software (any previous image) at any time. It also makes your automated testing more effective, as an immutable image that passes your tests in the test environment is likely to behave exactly the same way in the production environment.

Of course, it's possible to force configuration management tools to do immutable deployments too, but it's not the idiomatic approach for those tools, whereas it's a natural way to use provisioning tools. It's also worth mentioning that the immutable approach has downsides of its own. For example, rebuilding an image from a server template and redeploying all your servers for a trivial change can take a long time. Moreover, immutability only lasts until you actually run the image. Once a server is up and running, it'll start making changes on the hard drive and experiencing some degree of configuration drift (although this is mitigated if you deploy frequently).

Procedural Language Versus Declarative Language

Chef and Ansible encourage a *procedural* style where you write code that specifies, step by step, how to achieve some desired end state. Terraform, CloudFormation, SaltStack, Puppet, and Open Stack Heat all encourage a more *declarative* style where you write code that specifies your desired end state, and the IAC tool itself is responsible for figuring out how to achieve that state.

To demonstrate the difference, let's go through an example. Imagine you wanted to deploy 10 servers ("EC2 Instances" in AWS lingo) to run an AMI with ID ami-40d28157 (Ubuntu 16.04). Here is a simplified example of an Ansible template that does this using a procedural approach:

```
- ec2:
    count: 10
    image: ami-40d28157
    instance_type: t2.micro
```

And here is a simplified example of a Terraform configuration that does the same thing using a declarative approach:

```
resource "aws_instance" "example" {
  count         = 10
  ami           = "ami-40d28157"
  instance_type = "t2.micro"
}
```

Now at the surface, these two approaches may look similar, and when you initially execute them with Ansible or Terraform, they will produce similar results. The interesting thing is what happens when you want to make a change.

For example, imagine traffic has gone up and you want to increase the number of servers to 15. With Ansible, the procedural code you wrote earlier is no longer useful; if you just updated the number of servers to 15 and reran that code, it would deploy 15 new servers, giving you 25 total! So instead, you have to be aware of what is already deployed and write a totally new procedural script to add the 5 new servers:

```
- ec2:
    count: 5
    image: ami-40d28157
    instance_type: t2.micro
```

With declarative code, since all you do is declare the end state you want, and Terraform figures out how to get to that end state, Terraform will also be aware of any state it created in the past. Therefore, to deploy 5 more servers, all you have to do is go back to the same Terraform configuration and update the count from 10 to 15:

```
resource "aws_instance" "example" {
  count         = 15
  ami           = "ami-40d28157"
  instance_type = "t2.micro"
}
```

If you applied this configuration, Terraform would realize it had already created 10 servers and therefore that all it needed to do was create 5 new servers. In fact, before applying this configuration, you can use Terraform's plan command to preview what changes it would make:

```
> terraform plan

+ aws_instance.example.11
    ami:                 "ami-40d28157"
    instance_type:       "t2.micro"
+ aws_instance.example.12
    ami:                 "ami-40d28157"
    instance_type:       "t2.micro"
+ aws_instance.example.13
    ami:                 "ami-40d28157"
    instance_type:       "t2.micro"
+ aws_instance.example.14
    ami:                 "ami-40d28157"
    instance_type:       "t2.micro"
+ aws_instance.example.15
    ami:                 "ami-40d28157"
    instance_type:       "t2.micro"

Plan: 5 to add, 0 to change, 0 to destroy.
```

Now what happens when you want to deploy a different version of the app, such as AMI ID ami-408c7f28? With the procedural approach, both of your previous Ansible templates are again not useful, so you have to write yet another template to track down the 10 servers you deployed previously (or was it 15 now?) and carefully update each one to the new version. With the declarative approach of Terraform, you go back to the exact same configuration file once again and simply change the ami parameter to ami-408c7f28:

```
resource "aws_instance" "example" {
  count         = 15
  ami           = "ami-408c7f28"
  instance_type = "t2.micro"
}
```

Obviously, these examples are simplified. Ansible does allow you to use tags to search for existing EC2 Instances before deploying new ones (e.g., using the instance_tags and count_tag parameters), but having to manually figure out this sort of logic for every single resource you manage with Ansible, based on each resource's past history, can be surprisingly complicated (e.g., finding existing instances not only by tag, but also image version, availability zone, etc.). This highlights two major problems with procedural IAC tools:

1. *Procedural code does* not *fully capture the state of the infrastructure.* Reading through the three preceding Ansible templates is not enough to know what's deployed. You'd also have to know the *order* in which those templates were applied. Had you applied them in a different order, you might have ended up with different infrastructure, and that's not something you can see in the code

base itself. In other words, to reason about an Ansible or Chef codebase, you have to know the full history of every change that has ever happened.

2. *Procedural code limits reusability.* The reusability of procedural code is inherently limited because you have to manually take into account the current state of the infrastructure. Since that state is constantly changing, code you used a week ago may no longer be usable because it was designed to modify a state of your infrastructure that no longer exists. As a result, procedural codebases tend to grow large and complicated over time.

With Terraform's declarative approach, the code always represents the latest state of your infrastructure. At a glance, you can tell what's currently deployed and how it's configured, without having to worry about history or timing. This also makes it easy to create reusable code, as you don't have to manually account for the current state of the world. Instead, you just focus on describing your desired state, and Terraform figures out how to get from one state to the other automatically. As a result, Terraform codebases tend to stay small and easy to understand.

Of course, there are downsides to declarative languages too. Without access to a full programming language, your expressive power is limited. For example, some types of infrastructure changes, such as a zero-downtime deployment, are hard to express in purely declarative terms (but not impossible, as you'll see in Chapter 5). Similarly, without the ability to do "logic" (e.g., if-statements, loops), creating generic, reusable code can be tricky. Fortunately, Terraform provides a number of powerful primitives —such as input variables, output variables, modules, `create_before_destroy`, `count`, ternary syntax, and interpolation functions—that make it possible to create clean, configurable, modular code even in a declarative language. I'll come back to these topics in Chapter 4 and Chapter 5.

Master Versus Masterless

By default, Chef, Puppet, and SaltStack all require that you run a *master server* for storing the state of your infrastructure and distributing updates. Every time you want to update something in your infrastructure, you use a client (e.g., a command-line tool) to issue new commands to the master server, and the master server either pushes the updates out to all the other servers, or those servers pull the latest updates down from the master server on a regular basis.

A master server offers a few advantages. First, it's a single, central place where you can see and manage the status of your infrastructure. Many configuration management tools even provide a web interface (e.g., the Chef Console, Puppet Enterprise Console) for the master server to make it easier to see what's going on. Second, some master servers can run continuously in the background, and enforce your configuration. That way, if someone makes a manual change on a server, the master server can revert that change to prevent configuration drift.

However, having to run a master server has some serious drawbacks:

Extra infrastructure
You have to deploy an extra server, or even a cluster of extra servers (for high availability and scalability), just to run the master.

Maintenance
You have to maintain, upgrade, back up, monitor, and scale the master server(s).

Security
You have to provide a way for the client to communicate to the master server(s) and a way for the master server(s) to communicate with all the other servers, which typically means opening extra ports and configuring extra authentication systems, all of which increases your surface area to attackers.

Chef, Puppet, and SaltStack do have varying levels of support for masterless modes where you just run their agent software on each of your servers, typically on a periodic schedule (e.g., a cron job that runs every 5 minutes), and use that to pull down the latest updates from version control (rather than from a master server). This significantly reduces the number of moving parts, but, as discussed in the next section, this still leaves a number of unanswered questions, especially about how to provision the servers and install the agent software on them in the first place.

Ansible, CloudFormation, Heat, and Terraform are all masterless by default. Or, to be more accurate, some of them may rely on a master server, but it's already part of the infrastructure you're using and not an extra piece you have to manage. For example, Terraform communicates with cloud providers using the cloud provider's APIs, so in some sense, the API servers are master servers, except they don't require any extra infrastructure or any extra authentication mechanisms (i.e., just use your API keys). Ansible works by connecting directly to each server over SSH, so again, you don't have to run any extra infrastructure or manage extra authentication mechanisms (i.e., just use your SSH keys).

Agent Versus Agentless

Chef, Puppet, and SaltStack all require you to install *agent software* (e.g., Chef Client, Puppet Agent, Salt Minion) on each server you want to configure. The agent typically runs in the background on each server and is responsible for installing the latest configuration management updates.

This has a few drawbacks:

Bootstrapping
How do you provision your servers and install the agent software on them in the first place? Some configuration management tools kick the can down the road, assuming some external process will take care of this for them (e.g., you first use

Terraform to deploy a bunch of servers with an AMI that has the agent already installed); other configuration management tools have a special bootstrapping process where you run one-off commands to provision the servers using the cloud provider APIs and install the agent software on those servers over SSH.

Maintenance

You have to carefully update the agent software on a periodic basis, being careful to keep it in sync with the master server if there is one. You also have to monitor the agent software and restart it if it crashes.

Security

If the agent software pulls down configuration from a master server (or some other server if you're not using a master), then you have to open outbound ports on every server. If the master server pushes configuration to the agent, then you have to open inbound ports on every server. In either case, you have to figure out how to authenticate the agent to the server it's talking to. All of this increases your surface area to attackers.

Once again, Chef, Puppet, and SaltStack do have varying levels of support for agent-less modes (e.g., salt-ssh), but these always feel like they were tacked on as an after-thought and don't support the full feature set of the configuration management tool. That's why in the wild, the default or idiomatic configuration for Chef, Puppet, and SaltStack almost always includes an agent and usually a master too, as shown in Figure 1-7.

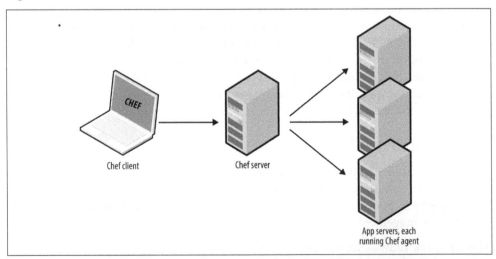

Figure 1-7. The typical architecture for Chef, Puppet, and SaltStack involves many moving parts. For example, the default setup for Chef is to run the Chef client on your computer, which talks to a Chef master server, which deploys changes by talking to Chef agents running on all your other servers.

All of these extra moving parts introduce a large number of new failure modes into your infrastructure. Each time you get a bug report at 3 a.m., you'll have to figure out if it's a bug in your application code, or your IAC code, or the configuration management client, or the master server(s), or the way the client talks to the master server(s), or the way other servers talk to the master server(s), or…

Ansible, CloudFormation, Heat, and Terraform do not require you to install any extra agents. Or, to be more accurate, some of them require agents, but these are typically already installed as part of the infrastructure you're using. For example, AWS, Azure, Google Cloud, and all other cloud providers take care of installing, managing, and authenticating agent software on each of their physical servers. As a user of Terraform, you don't have to worry about any of that: you just issue commands and the cloud provider's agents execute them for you on all of your servers, as shown in Figure 1-8. With Ansible, your servers need to run the SSH Daemon, which is common to run on most servers anyway.

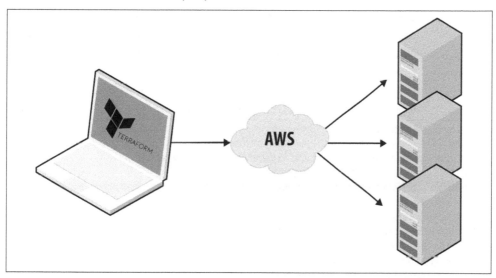

Figure 1-8. Terraform uses a masterless, agent-only architecture. All you need to run is the Terraform client and it takes care of the rest by using the APIs of cloud providers, such as AWS.

Large Community Versus Small Community

Whenever you pick a technology, you are also picking a community. In many cases, the ecosystem around the project can have a bigger impact on your experience than the inherent quality of the technology itself. The community determines how many people contribute to the project, how many plug-ins, integrations, and extensions are available, how easy it is to find help online (e.g., blog posts, questions on StackOverflow), and how easy it is to hire someone to help you (e.g., an employee, consultant, or support company).

It's hard to do an accurate comparison between communities, but you can spot some trends by searching online. Table 1-1 shows a comparison of popular IAC tools from September 2016, including whether they are open source or closed source, what cloud providers they support, the total number of contributors and stars on GitHub, how many active changes and issues there were in the month of September, how many open source libraries are available for the tool, the number of questions listed for that tool on StackOverflow, and the number of jobs that mention the tool on Indeed.com.[8]

Table 1-1. A comparison of IAC communities

	Source	Cloud	Contributors	Stars	Commits in Sept	Bugs in Sept	Libraries	StackOverflow	Jobs
Chef	Open	All	477	4,439	182	58	3,052[a]	4,187	5,631[b]
Puppet	Open	All	432	4,158	79	130[c]	4,435[d]	2,639	5,213[e]
Ansible	Open	All	1,488	18,895	340	315	8,044[f]	3,633	3,901
SaltStack	Open	All	1,596	6,897	689	347	240[g]	614	454
CloudFormation	Closed	AWS	?	?	?	?	240[h]	613	665
Heat	Open	All	283	283	83	36[i]	0[j]	52	72[k]
Terraform	Open	All	653	5,732	440	480	40[l]	131	392

[a] This is the number of cookbooks in the Chef Supermarket (*https://supermarket.chef.io/cookbooks*).
[b] To avoid false positives for the term "chef", I searched for "chef engineer".
[c] Based on the Puppet Labs JIRA account (*https://tickets.puppetlabs.com/secure/Dashboard.jspa*).
[d] This is the number of modules in the Puppet Forge (*https://forge.puppet.com*).
[e] To avoid false positives for the term "puppet", I searched for "puppet engineer".
[f] This is the number of reusable roles in Ansible Galaxy (*https://galaxy.ansible.com*).
[g] This is the number of formulas in the Salt Stack Formulas GitHub account (*https://github.com/saltstack-formulas*).
[h] This is the number of templates in the awslabs GitHub account (*https://github.com/awslabs*).
[i] Based on the OpenStack bug tracker (*https://bugs.launchpad.net/openstack*).
[j] I could not find any collections of community Heat templates.
[k] To avoid false positives for the term "heat", I searched for "openstack".
[l] This is the number of modules in the terraform-community-modules repo (*https://github.com/terraform-community-modules*).

Obviously, this is not a perfect apples-to-apples comparison. For example, some of the tools have more than one repository, and some use other methods for bug tracking and questions; searching for jobs with common words like "chef" or "puppet" is tricky; and so on.

---

8 Most of this data, including the number of contributors, stars, changes, and issues, comes from the open source repositories and bug trackers for each tool. Since CloudFormation is closed source, some of this information is not available.

That said, a few trends are obvious. First, all of the IAC tools in this comparison are open source and work with many cloud providers, except for CloudFormation, which is closed source, and only works with AWS. Second, Chef, Puppet, and Ansible seem to be the most popular tools, although SaltStack and Terraform aren't too far behind.

Mature Versus Cutting Edge

Another key factor to consider when picking any technology is maturity. Table 1-2 shows the initial release dates and current version number (as of January 2017) for of each of the IAC tools.

Table 1-2. A comparison of IAC maturity

	Initial release	Current version
Puppet	2005	4.8.1
Chef	2009	12.17.44
CloudFormation	2011	?
SaltStack	2011	2016.11.1
Ansible	2012	v2.1.3.0-1
Heat	2012	7.0.1
Terraform	2014	0.8.2

Again, this is not an apples-to-apples comparison, since different tools have different versioning schemes, but some trends are clear. Terraform is, by far, the youngest IAC tool in this comparison. It's still pre 1.0.0, so there is no guarantee of a stable or backward compatible API, and bugs are relatively common (although most of them are minor). This is Terraform's biggest weakness: although it has gotten extremely popular in a short time, the price you pay for using this new, cutting-edge tool is that it is not as mature as some of the other IAC options.

Conclusion

Putting it all together, Table 1-3 shows how the most popular IAC tools stack up. Note that this table shows the *default* or *most common* way the various IAC tools are used, though as discussed earlier in this chapter, these IAC tools are flexible enough to be used in other configurations, too (e.g., Chef can be used without a master, Salt can be used to do immutable infrastructure).

Table 1-3. A comparison of the most common way to use the most popular IAC tools

	Source	Cloud	Type	Infrastructure	Language	Agent	Master	Community	Maturity
Chef	Open	All	Config Mgmt	Mutable	Procedural	Yes	Yes	Large	High
Puppet	Open	All	Config Mgmt	Mutable	Declarative	Yes	Yes	Large	High
Ansible	Open	All	Config Mgmt	Mutable	Procedural	No	No	Large	Medium
SaltStack	Open	All	Config Mgmt	Mutable	Declarative	Yes	Yes	Medium	Medium
CloudFormation	Closed	AWS	Provisioning	Immutable	Declarative	No	No	Small	Medium
Heat	Open	All	Provisioning	Immutable	Declarative	No	No	Small	Low
Terraform	Open	All	Provisioning	Immutable	Declarative	No	No	Medium	Low

At Gruntwork, what we wanted was an open source, cloud-agnostic provisioning tool that supported immutable infrastructure, a declarative language, a masterless and agentless architecture, and had a large community and a mature codebase. Table 1-3 shows that Terraform, while not perfect, comes the closest to meeting all of our criteria.

Does Terraform fit your criteria, too? If so, then head over to Chapter 2 to learn how to use it.

## CHAPTER 2

Getting Started with Terraform

In this chapter, you're going to learn the basics of how to use Terraform. It's an easy tool to learn, so in the span of about 30 pages, you'll go from running your first Terraform commands all the way up to using Terraform to deploy a cluster of servers with a load balancer that distributes traffic across them. This infrastructure is a good starting point for running scalable, highly available web services and microservices. In subsequent chapters, you'll evolve this example even further.

Terraform can provision infrastructure across public cloud providers such as Amazon Web Services (AWS), Azure, Google Cloud, and DigitalOcean, as well as private cloud and virtualization platforms such as OpenStack and VMWare. For just about all of the code examples in this chapter and the rest of the book, you are going to use AWS. AWS is a good choice for learning Terraform because:

- AWS is the most popular cloud infrastructure provider, by far. It has a 45% share in the cloud infrastructure market, which is more than the next three biggest competitors (Microsoft, Google, and IBM) combined (*http://bit.ly/2kWCuCm*).

- AWS provides a huge range of reliable and scalable cloud hosting services, including: Elastic Compute Cloud (EC2), which you can use to deploy virtual servers; Auto Scaling Groups (ASGs), which make it easier to manage a cluster of virtual servers; and Elastic Load Balancers (ELBs), which you can use to distribute traffic across the cluster of virtual servers.[1]

- AWS offers a generous Free Tier (*https://aws.amazon.com/free/*) that should allow you to run all of these examples for free. If you already used up your free tier

---

[1] If you find the AWS terminology confusing, be sure to check out AWS in Plain English (*https://www.expeditedssl.com/aws-in-plain-english*).

credits, the examples in this book should still cost you no more than a few dollars.

If you've never used AWS or Terraform before, don't worry, as this tutorial is designed for novices to both technologies. I'll walk you through the following steps:

- Set up your AWS account
- Install Terraform
- Deploy a single server
- Deploy a single web server
- Deploy a configurable web server
- Deploy a cluster of web servers
- Deploy a load balancer
- Clean up

 Example Code

As a reminder, all of the code examples in the book can be found at the following URL: *https://github.com/brikis98/terraform-up-and-running-code*.

Set Up Your AWS Account

If you don't already have an AWS account, head over to *https://aws.amazon.com* and sign up. When you first register for AWS, you initially sign in as *root user*. This user account has access permissions to do absolutely anything in the account, so from a security perspective, it's not a good idea to use the root user on a day-to-day basis. In fact, the *only* thing you should use the root user for is to create other user accounts with more limited permissions, and switch to one of those accounts immediately.[2]

To create a more limited user account, you will need to use the *Identity and Access Management (IAM)* service. IAM is where you manage user accounts as well as the permissions for each user. To create a new *IAM user*, head over to the IAM Console (*https://console.aws.amazon.com/iam/*), click "Users," and click the blue "Create New Users" button. Enter a name for the user and make sure "Generate an access key for each user" is checked, as shown in Figure 2-1.

---

2 For more details on AWS user management best practices, see *http://amzn.to/2lvJ8Rf*.

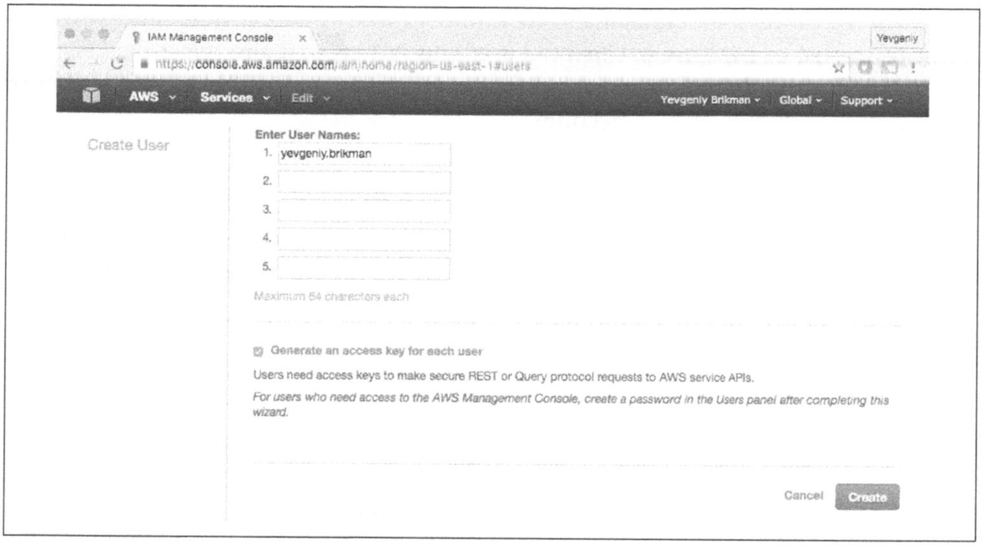

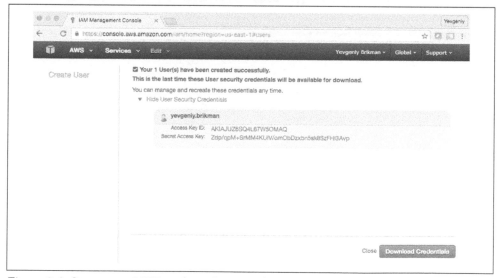

Figure 2-1. Create a new IAM user

Click the "Create" button and AWS will show you the security credentials for that user, which consist of an *Access Key ID* and a *Secret Access Key*, as shown in Figure 2-2. You must save these immediately, as they will never be shown again. I recommend storing them somewhere secure (e.g., a password manager such as 1Password, LastPass, or OS X Keychain) so you can use them a little later in this tutorial.

Figure 2-2. Store your AWS credentials somewhere secure. Never share them with anyone. Don't worry, the ones in the screenshot are fake.

Once you've saved your credentials, click the "Close" button (twice), and you'll be taken to the list of IAM users. Click the user you just created and select the "Permissions" tab. By default, new IAM users have no permissions whatsoever, and therefore cannot do anything in an AWS account.

To give an IAM user permissions to do something, you need to associate one or more IAM Policies with that user's account. An *IAM Policy* is a JSON document that defines what a user is or isn't allowed to do. You can create your own IAM Policies or use some of the predefined IAM Policies, which are known as *Managed Policies*.[3]

To run the examples in this book, you will need to add the following Managed Policies to your IAM user, as shown in Figure 2-3:

1. `AmazonEC2FullAccess`: required for this chapter.

2. `AmazonS3FullAccess`: required for Chapter 3.

3. `AmazonDynamoDBFullAccess`: required for Chapter 3.

4. `AmazonRDSFullAccess`: required for Chapter 3.

5. `CloudWatchFullAccess`: required for Chapter 5.

6. `IAMFullAccess`: required for Chapter 5.

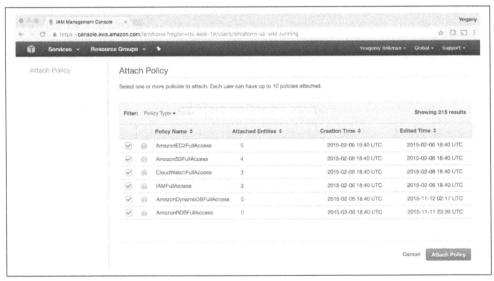

Figure 2-3. Add several Managed IAM Policies to your new IAM user

---

3 You can learn more about IAM Policies here: *http://amzn.to/2lQs1MA*.

A Note on Default VPCs

Please note that if you are using an existing AWS account, it must have a *Default VPC* in it. A *VPC*, or Virtual Private Cloud, is an isolated area of your AWS account that has its own virtual network and IP address space. Just about every AWS resource deploys into a VPC. If you don't explicitly specify a VPC, the resource will be deployed into the *Default VPC*, which is part of every new AWS account. All the examples in this book rely on this Default VPC, so if for some reason you deleted the one in your account, either use a different region (each region has its own Default VPC) or contact AWS customer support, and they can re-create a Default VPC for you (there is no way to mark a VPC as "Default" yourself). Otherwise, you'll need to update almost every example to include a vpc_id or subnet_id parameter pointing to a custom VPC.

Install Terraform

You can download Terraform from the Terraform homepage (*https://www.terra form.io*). Click the download link, select the appropriate package for your operating system, download the zip archive, and unzip it into the directory where you want Terraform to be installed. The archive will extract a single binary called terraform, which you'll want to add to your PATH environment variable.

To check if things are working, run the terraform command, and you should see the usage instructions:

```
> terraform
usage: terraform [--version] [--help] <command> [<args>]

Available commands are:
    apply       Builds or changes infrastructure
    destroy     Destroy Terraform-managed infrastructure
    get         Download and install modules for the configuration
    graph       Create a visual graph of Terraform resources
    (...)
```

In order for Terraform to be able to make changes in your AWS account, you will need to set the AWS credentials for the IAM user you created earlier as the environment variables AWS_ACCESS_KEY_ID and AWS_SECRET_ACCESS_KEY. For example, here is how you can do it in a Unix/Linux/OS X terminal:

```
> export AWS_ACCESS_KEY_ID=(your access key id)
> export AWS_SECRET_ACCESS_KEY=(your secret access key)
```

Note that these environment variables will only apply to the current shell, so if you reboot your computer or open a new terminal window, you'll have to export these variables again.

Authentication Options

In addition to environment variables, Terraform supports the same authentication mechanisms as all AWS CLI and SDK tools. Therefore, it'll also be able to use credentials in *$HOME/.aws/credentials*, which are automatically generated if you run the `configure` command on the AWS CLI, or IAM Roles, which you can add to almost any resource in AWS. For more info, see Configuring the AWS Command Line Interface (*http://docs.aws.amazon.com/cli/latest/userguide/cli-chap-getting-started.html*).

Deploy a Single Server

Terraform code is written in the *HashiCorp Configuration Language (HCL)* in files with the extension *.tf*.[4] It is a declarative language, so your goal is to describe the infrastructure you want, and Terraform will figure out how to create it. Terraform can create infrastructure across a wide variety of platforms, or what it calls *providers*, including AWS, Azure, Google Cloud, DigitalOcean, and many others.

You can write Terraform code in just about any text editor. If you search around, you can find Terraform syntax highlighting support for most editors (note, you may have to search for the word "HCL" instead of "Terraform"), including vim, emacs, Sublime Text, Atom, Visual Studio Code, and IntelliJ (the latter even has support for refactoring, find usages, and go to declaration).

The first step to using Terraform is typically to configure the provider(s) you want to use. Create an empty folder and put a file in it called *main.tf* with the following contents:

```
provider "aws" {
  region = "us-east-1"
}
```

This tells Terraform that you are going to be using AWS as your provider and that you wish to deploy your infrastructure into the `us-east-1` region. AWS has data centers all over the world, grouped into regions and availability zones. An *AWS region* is a separate geographic area, such as `us-east-1` (North Virginia), `eu-west-1` (Ireland), and `ap-southeast-2` (Sydney). Within each region, there are multiple isolated data centers known as *availability zones*, such as `us-east-1a`, `us-east-1b`, and so on.[5]

For each type of provider, there are many different kinds of *resources* you can create, such as servers, databases, and load balancers. For example, to deploy a single server

---

4 You can also write Terraform code in pure JSON in files with the extension *.tf.json*. You can learn more about Terraform's HCL and JSON syntax here: *https://www.terraform.io/docs/configuration/syntax.html*.

5 You can learn more about AWS regions and availability zones here: *http://bit.ly/1NATGqS*.

in AWS, known as an EC2 Instance, you can add the `aws_instance` resource to *main.tf*:

```
resource "aws_instance" "example" {
  ami           = "ami-40d28157"
  instance_type = "t2.micro"
}
```

The general syntax for a Terraform resource is:

```
resource "PROVIDER_TYPE" "NAME" {
  [CONFIG ...]
}
```

where PROVIDER is the name of a provider (e.g., aws), TYPE is the type of resources to create in that provider (e.g., instance), NAME is an identifier you can use throughout the Terraform code to refer to this resource (e.g., example), and CONFIG consists of one or more configuration parameters that are specific to that resource (e.g., ami = "ami-40d28157"). For the `aws_instance` resource, there are many different configuration parameters, but for now, you only need to set the following ones:[6]

ami

The Amazon Machine Image (AMI) to run on the EC2 Instance. You can find free and paid AMIs in the AWS Marketplace (*https://aws.amazon.com/market place/*) or create your own using tools such as Packer (see "Server Templating Tools" on page 7 for a discussion of machine images and server templating). The preceding code example sets the ami parameter to the ID of an Ubuntu 16.04 AMI in us-east-1.

instance_type

The type of EC2 Instance to run. Each type of EC2 Instance provides a different amount CPU, memory, disk space, and networking capacity. The EC2 Instance Types (*https://aws.amazon.com/ec2/instance-types/*) page lists all the available options. The preceding example uses t2.micro, which has one virtual CPU, 1GB of memory, and is part of the AWS free tier.

In a terminal, go into the folder where you created *main.tf*, and run the `terraform plan` command:

```
> terraform plan

Refreshing Terraform state in-memory prior to plan...
(...)
```

---

6 You can find the full list of aws_instance configuration parameters here: *https://www.terraform.io/docs/providers/aws/r/instance.html*.

```
+ aws_instance.example
    ami:                         "ami-40d28157"
    availability_zone:           "<computed>"
    instance_state:              "<computed>"
    instance_type:               "t2.micro"
    key_name:                    "<computed>"
    private_dns:                 "<computed>"
    private_ip:                  "<computed>"
    public_dns:                  "<computed>"
    public_ip:                   "<computed>"
    security_groups.#:           "<computed>"
    subnet_id:                   "<computed>"
    vpc_security_group_ids.#:    "<computed>"
    (...)

Plan: 1 to add, 0 to change, 0 to destroy.
```

The plan command lets you see what Terraform will do before actually making any changes. This is a great way to sanity check your code before unleashing it onto the world. The output of the plan command is similar to the output of the diff command that is part of Unix, Linux, and git: resources with a plus sign (+) are going to be created, resources with a minus sign (–) are going to be deleted, and resources with a tilde sign (~) are going to be modified. In the preceding output, you can see that Terraform is planning on creating a single EC2 Instance and nothing else, which is exactly what you want.

To actually create the instance, run the terraform apply command:

```
> terraform apply

aws_instance.example: Creating...
    ami:                         "" => "ami-40d28157"
    availability_zone:           "" => "<computed>"
    instance_state:              "" => "<computed>"
    instance_type:               "" => "t2.micro"
    key_name:                    "" => "<computed>"
    private_dns:                 "" => "<computed>"
    private_ip:                  "" => "<computed>"
    public_dns:                  "" => "<computed>"
    public_ip:                   "" => "<computed>"
    security_groups.#:           "" => "<computed>"
    subnet_id:                   "" => "<computed>"
    vpc_security_group_ids.#:    "" => "<computed>"
    (...)

aws_instance.example: Still creating... (10s elapsed)
aws_instance.example: Still creating... (20s elapsed)
aws_instance.example: Creation complete

Apply complete! Resources: 1 added, 0 changed, 0 destroyed.
```

Congrats, you've just deployed a server with Terraform! To verify this, head over to the EC2 console (*https://console.aws.amazon.com/ec2/v2/home*), and you should see something similar to Figure 2-4.

Figure 2-4. A single EC2 Instance

Sure enough the server is there, though admittedly, this isn't the most exciting example. Let's make it a bit more interesting. First, notice that the EC2 Instance doesn't have a name. To add one, you can add `tags` to the `aws_instance` resource:

```
resource "aws_instance" "example" {
  ami           = "ami-40d28157"
  instance_type = "t2.micro"

  tags {
    Name = "terraform-example"
  }
}
```

Run the `plan` command again to see what this would do:

```
> terraform plan

aws_instance.example: Refreshing state... (ID: i-6a7c545b)
(...)

~ aws_instance.example
    tags.%:     "0" => "1"
    tags.Name:  "" => "terraform-example"

Plan: 0 to add, 1 to change, 0 to destroy.
```

Terraform keeps track of all the resources it already created for this set of configuration files, so it knows your EC2 Instance already exists (notice Terraform says "Refreshing state..." when you run the `plan` command), and it can show you a diff between what's currently deployed and what's in your Terraform code (this is one of the advantages of using a declarative language over a procedural one, as discussed in "How Terraform Compares to Other Infrastructure as Code Tools" on page 17). The preceding diff shows that Terraform wants to create a single tag called "Name," which is exactly what you need, so run the `apply` command again.

When you refresh your EC2 console, you'll see something similar to Figure 2-5.

Figure 2-5. The EC2 Instance now has a name tag

Now that you have some working Terraform code, you may want to store it in version control. This allows you to share your code with other team members, track the history of all infrastructure changes, and use the commit log for debugging. For example, here is how you can create a local Git repository and use it to store your Terraform configuration file:

```
git init
git add main.tf
git commit -m "Initial commit"
```

You should also create a file called *.gitignore* that tells Git to ignore certain types of files so you don't accidentally check them in:

```
.terraform
*.tfstate
*.tfstate.backup
```

The preceding *.gitignore* file tells Git to ignore the *.terraform* folder, which Terraform uses as a temporary scratch directory, as well as *.tfstate* files, which Terraform uses to store state (In Chapter 3, you'll see why state files shouldn't be checked in). You should commit the *.gitignore* file, too:

```
git add .gitignore
git commit -m "Add a .gitignore file"
```

To share this code with your teammates, you'll want to create a shared Git repository that you can all access. One way to do this is to use GitHub. Head over to github.com, create an account if you don't have one already, and create a new repository. Configure your local Git repository to use the new GitHub repository as a remote endpoint named origin as follows:

```
git remote add origin git@github.com:<YOUR_USERNAME>/<YOUR_REPO_NAME>.git
```

Now, whenever you want to share your commits with your teammates, you can *push* them to origin:

```
git push origin master
```

And whenever you want to see changes your teammates have made, you can *pull* them from origin:

```
git pull origin master
```

As you go through the rest of this book, and as you use Terraform in general, make sure to regularly git commit and git push your changes. This way, you'll not only be able to collaborate with team members on this code, but all your infrastructure changes will also be captured in the commit log, which is very handy for debugging. You'll learn more about using Terraform as a team in Chapter 6.

Deploy a Single Web Server

The next step is to run a web server on this Instance. The goal is to deploy the simplest web architecture possible: a single web server that can respond to HTTP requests, as shown in Figure 2-6.

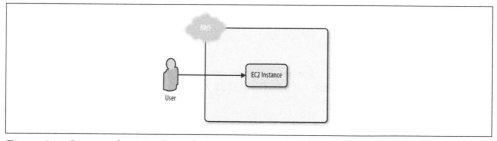

Figure 2-6. Start with a simple architecture: a single web server running in AWS that responds to HTTP requests

In a real-world use case, you'd probably build the web server using a web framework like Ruby on Rails or Django, but to keep this example simple, let's run a dirt-simple web server that always returns the text "Hello, World":[7]

```
#!/bin/bash
echo "Hello, World" > index.html
nohup busybox httpd -f -p 8080 &
```

This is a Bash script that writes the text "Hello, World" into *index.html* and runs a tool called busybox (*https://busybox.net/*) (which is installed by default on Ubuntu) to fire up a web server on port 8080 to serve that file. I wrapped the busybox command with nohup and & so that the web server runs permanently in the background, while the Bash script itself can exit.

Port Numbers

The reason this example uses port 8080, rather than the default HTTP port 80, is that listening on any port less than 1024 requires root user privileges. This is a security risk, because any attacker who manages to compromise your server would get root privileges, too.

Therefore, it's a best practice to run your web server with a non-root user that has limited permissions. That means you have to listen on higher-numbered ports, but as you'll see later in this chapter, you can configure a load balancer to listen on port 80 and route traffic to the high-numbered ports on your server(s).

How do you get the EC2 Instance to run this script? Normally, as discussed in "Server Templating Tools" on page 7, you would use a tool like Packer to create a custom AMI that has the web server installed on it. Since the dummy web server in this example is just a one-liner that uses busybox, you can use a plain Ubuntu 16.04 AMI, and run the "Hello, World" script as part of the EC2 Instance's *User Data* configuration, which AWS will execute when the Instance is booting:

```
resource "aws_instance" "example" {
  ami           = "ami-40d28157"
  instance_type = "t2.micro"

  user_data = <<-EOF
              #!/bin/bash
              echo "Hello, World" > index.html
              nohup busybox httpd -f -p 8080 &
              EOF
```

---

7 You can find a handy list of HTTP server one-liners here: *https://gist.github.com/willurd/5720255.*

```
  tags {
    Name = "terraform-example"
  ]
}
```

The <<-EOF and EOF are Terraform's *heredoc* syntax, which allows you to create multi-line strings without having to insert newline characters all over the place.

You need to do one more thing before this web server works. By default, AWS does not allow any incoming or outgoing traffic from an EC2 Instance. To allow the EC2 Instance to receive traffic on port 8080, you need to create a *security group*:

```
resource "aws_security_group" "instance" {
  name = "terraform-example-instance"

  ingress {
    from_port   = 8080
    to_port     = 8080
    protocol    = "tcp"
    cidr_blocks = ["0.0.0.0/0"]
  }
}
```

This code creates a new resource called aws_security_group (notice how all resources for the AWS provider start with aws_) and specifies that this group allows incoming TCP requests on port 8080 from the CIDR block 0.0.0.0/0. *CIDR blocks* are a concise way to specify IP address ranges. For example, a CIDR block of 10.0.0.0/24 represents all IP addresses between 10.0.0.0 and 10.0.0.255. The CIDR block 0.0.0.0/0 is an IP address range that includes all possible IP addresses, so this security group allows incoming requests on port 8080 from any IP.[8]

Simply creating a security group isn't enough; you also need to tell the EC2 Instance to actually use it. To do that, you need to pass the ID of the security group into the vpc_security_group_ids parameter of the aws_instance resource.

To get the ID of the security group, you can use *interpolation syntax*, which looks like this:

```
"${something_to_interpolate}"
```

Whenever you see a dollar sign and curly braces inside of double quotes, that means Terraform is going to process the text within the curly braces in a special way. You'll see many different uses for this syntax throughout the book. The first use will be to look up an *attribute* of a resource.

---

8 To learn more about how CIDR works, see *http://bit.ly/2l8Ki9g*. For a handy calculator that converts between IP address ranges and CIDR notation, see *http://www.ipaddressguide.com/cidr*.

In Terraform, every resource exposes attributes that you can access using interpolation (you can find the list of available attributes in the documentation for each resource). The syntax is:

```
"${TYPE.NAME.ATTRIBUTE}"
```

For example, here is how you can get the ID of the security group:

```
"${aws_security_group.instance.id}"
```

You can use this security group ID in the vpc_security_group_ids parameter of the aws_instance:

```
resource "aws_instance" "example" {
  ami           = "ami-40d28157"
  instance_type = "t2.micro"
  vpc_security_group_ids = ["${aws_security_group.instance.id}"]

  user_data = <<-EOF
              #!/bin/bash
              echo "Hello, World" > index.html
              nohup busybox httpd -f -p 8080 &
              EOF

  tags {
    Name = "terraform-example"
  }
}
```

When you use interpolation syntax to have one resource reference another resource, you create an *implicit dependency*. Terraform parses these dependencies, builds a dependency graph from them, and uses that to automatically figure out in what order it should create resources. For example, Terraform knows it needs to create the security group before the EC2 Instance, since the EC2 Instance references the ID of the security group. You can even get Terraform to show you the dependency graph by running the graph command:

```
> terraform graph

digraph {
  compound = "true"
  newrank = "true"
  subgraph "root" {
    "[root] aws_instance.example"
      [label = "aws_instance.example", shape = "box"]
    "[root] aws_security_group.instance"
      [label = "aws_security_group.instance", shape = "box"]
    "[root] provider.aws"
      [label = "provider.aws", shape = "diamond"]
    "[root] aws_instance.example" -> "[root] aws_security_group.instance"
    "[root] aws_instance.example" -> "[root] provider.aws"
    "[root] aws_security_group.instance" -> "[root] provider.aws"
```

```
    }
  }
```

The output is in a graph description language called DOT, which you can turn into an image, such as the dependency graph in Figure 2-7, by using a desktop app such as Graphviz or webapp such as GraphvizOnline (*http://bit.ly/2mPbxmg*).

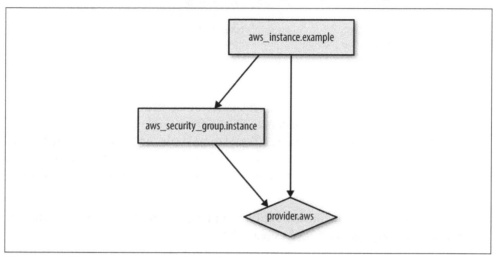

Figure 2-7. The dependency graph for the EC2 Instance and its security group

When Terraform walks your dependency tree, it will create as many resources in parallel as it can, which means it is very fast at applying your changes. That's the beauty of a declarative language: you just specify what you want and Terraform figures out the most efficient way to make it happen.

If you run the `plan` command, you'll see that Terraform wants to add a security group and replace the original EC2 Instance with a new one that has the new user data (the `-/+` means "replace"):

```
> terraform plan

(...)


+ aws_security_group.instance
    description:                          "Managed by Terraform"
    egress.#:                             "<computed>"
    ingress.#:                            "1"
    ingress.516175195.cidr_blocks.#:      "1"
    ingress.516175195.cidr_blocks.0:      "0.0.0.0/0"
    ingress.516175195.from_port:          "8080"
    ingress.516175195.protocol:           "tcp"
    ingress.516175195.security_groups.#:  "0"
    ingress.516175195.self:               "false"
```

```
    ingress.516175195.to_port:        "8080"
    owner_id:                         "<computed>"
    vpc_id:                           "<computed>"

-/+ aws_instance.example
    ami:                         "ami-40d28157" => "ami-40d28157"
    instance_state:              "running" => "<computed>"
    instance_type:               "t2.micro" => "t2.micro"
    security_groups.#:           "0" => "<computed>"
    vpc_security_group_ids.#:    "1" => "<computed>"
    (...)

Plan: 2 to add, 0 to change, 1 to destroy.
```

In Terraform, most changes to an EC2 Instance, other than metadata such as tags, actually create a completely new Instance. This is an example of the immutable infrastructure paradigm discussed in "Server Templating Tools" on page 7. It's worth mentioning that while the web server is being replaced, your users would experience downtime; you'll see how to do a zero-downtime deployment with Terraform in Chapter 5.

Since the plan looks good, run the apply command again and you'll see your new EC2 Instance deploying, as shown in Figure 2-8.

Figure 2-8. The new EC2 Instance with the web server code replaces the old Instance

In the description panel at the bottom of the screen, you'll also see the public IP address of this EC2 Instance. Give it a minute or two to boot up and then use a web browser or a tool like curl to make an HTTP request to this IP address at port 8080:

```
> curl http://<EC2_INSTANCE_PUBLIC_IP>:8080
Hello, World
```

Yay, you now have a working web server running in AWS!

Network Security

To keep all the examples in this book simple, they deploy not only into your Default VPC (as mentioned earlier), but also the default *subnets* of that VPC. A VPC is partitioned into one or more subnets, each with its own IP addresses. The subnets in the Default VPC are all *public subnets*, which means they get IP addresses that are accessible from the public internet. This is why you are able to test your EC2 Instance from your home computer.

Running a server in a public subnet is fine for a quick experiment, but in real-world usage, it's a security risk. Hackers all over the world are *constantly* scanning IP addresses at random for any weakness. If your servers are exposed publicly, all it takes is accidentally leaving a single port unprotected or running out-of-date code with a known vulnerability, and someone can break in.

Therefore, for production systems, you should deploy all of your servers, and certainly all of your data stores, in *private subnets*, which have IP addresses that can only be accessed from inside the VPC and not from the public internet. The only servers you should run in public subnets are a small number of reverse proxies and load balancers (you'll see an example of a load balancer later in this chapter) that you lock down as much as possible.

Deploy a Configurable Web Server

You may have noticed that the web server code has the port 8080 duplicated in both the security group and the User Data configuration. This violates the *Don't Repeat Yourself (DRY)* principle: every piece of knowledge must have a single, unambiguous, authoritative representation within a system.[9] If you have the port number copy/pasted in two places, it's too easy to update it in one place but forget to make the same change in the other place.

To allow you to make your code more DRY and more configurable, Terraform allows you to define *input variables*. The syntax for declaring a variable is:

```
variable "NAME" {
  [CONFIG ...]
}
```

---

9 From *The Pragmatic Programmer* by Andy Hunt and Dave Thomas (Addison-Wesley Professional).

The body of the variable declaration can contain three parameters, all of them optional:

description

It's always a good idea to use this parameter to document how a variable is used. Your teammates will not only be able to see this description while reading the code, but also when running the `plan` or `apply` commands (you'll see an example of this shortly).

default

There are a number of ways to provide a value for the variable, including passing it in at the command line (using the `-var` option), via a file (using the `-var-file` option), or via an environment variable (Terraform looks for environment variables of the name `TF_VAR_<variable_name>`). If no value is passed in, the variable will fall back to this default value. If there is no default value, Terraform will interactively prompt the user for one.

type

Must be one of `"string"`, `"list"`, or `"map"`. If you don't specify a type, Terraform will try to guess the type from the `default` value. If there is no `default`, then Terraform will assume the variable is a string.

Here is an example of a list input variable in Terraform:

```
variable "list_example" {
  description = "An example of a list in Terraform"
  type        = "list"
  default     = [1, 2, 3]
}
```

And here's a map:

```
variable "map_example" {
  description = "An example of a map in Terraform"
  type        = "map"

  default = {
    key1 = "value1"
    key2 = "value2"
    key3 = "value3"
  }
}
```

For the web server example, all you need is a number, which in Terraform, are automatically coerced to strings, so you can omit the type:[10]

```
variable "server_port" {
  description = "The port the server will use for HTTP requests"
}
```

Note that the `server_port` input variable has no `default`, so if you run the `plan` or `apply` command now, Terraform will prompt you to enter a value for it and show you the `description` of the variable:

```
> terraform plan

var.server_port
  The port the server will use for HTTP requests

Enter a value:
```

If you don't want to deal with an interactive prompt, you can provide a value for the variable via the `-var` command-line option:

```
> terraform plan -var server_port="8080"
```

And if you don't want to deal with remembering a command-line flag every time you run `plan` or `apply`, you're better off specifying a `default` value:

```
variable "server_port" {
  description = "The port the server will use for HTTP requests"
  default = 8080
}
```

To extract values from these input variables in your Terraform code, you can use interpolation syntax again. The syntax for looking up a variable is:

```
"${var.VARIABLE_NAME}"
```

For example, here is how you can set the `from_port` and `to_port` parameters of the security group to the value of the `server_port` variable:

```
resource "aws_security_group" "instance" {
  name = "terraform-example-instance"

  ingress {
    from_port   = "${var.server_port}"
    to_port     = "${var.server_port}"
    protocol    = "tcp"
    cidr_blocks = ["0.0.0.0/0"]
```

---

10 Terraform allows you to specify numbers and booleans without quotes around them, but under the hood, it converts them all to strings. Numbers are converted more or less as you'd expect, where a 1 becomes "1". Booleans are first converted to a number and then a string, so a `true` becomes "1" and a `false` becomes "0".

```
        }
    }
```

You can use the same syntax to set the port number used by busybox in the User Data of the EC2 Instance:

```
user_data = <<-EOF
            #!/bin/bash
            echo "Hello, World" > index.html
            nohup busybox httpd -f -p "${var.server_port}" &
            EOF
```

In addition to input variables, Terraform also allows you to define *ouput variables* with the following syntax:

```
output "NAME" {
  value = VALUE
}
```

For example, instead of having to manually poke around the EC2 console to find the IP address of your server, you can provide the IP address as an output variable:

```
output "public_ip" {
  value = "${aws_instance.example.public_ip}"
}
```

This code uses interpolation syntax again, this time to reference the `public_ip` attribute of the `aws_instance` resource. If you run the `apply` command again, Terraform will not apply any changes (since you haven't changed any resources), but it will show you the new output at the very end:

```
> terraform apply

aws_security_group.instance: Refreshing state... (ID: sg-db91dba1)
aws_instance.example: Refreshing state... (ID: i-61744350)

Apply complete! Resources: 0 added, 0 changed, 0 destroyed.

Outputs:

public_ip = 54.174.13.5
```

As you can see, output variables show up in the console after you run `terraform apply`. You can also use the `terraform output` command to list outputs without applying any changes and `terraform output OUTPUT_NAME` to see the value of a specific output:

```
> terraform output public_ip
54.174.13.5
```

Input and output variables are essential ingredients in creating configurable and reusable infrastructure code, a topic you'll see more of in Chapter 4.

Deploy a Cluster of Web Servers

Running a single server is a good start, but in the real world, a single server is a single point of failure. If that server crashes, or if it becomes overloaded from too much traffic, users will be unable to access your site. The solution is to run a cluster of servers, routing around servers that go down, and adjusting the size of the cluster up or down based on traffic.[11]

Managing such a cluster manually is a lot of work. Fortunately, you can let AWS take care of it for by you using an *Auto Scaling Group (ASG)*, as shown in Figure 2-9. An ASG takes care of a lot of tasks for you completely automatically, including launching a cluster of EC2 Instances, monitoring the health of each Instance, replacing failed Instances, and adjusting the size of the cluster in response to load.

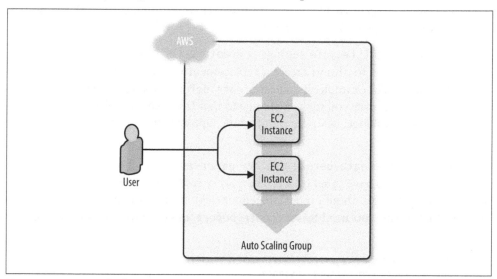

Figure 2-9. Instead of a single web server, run a cluster of web servers using an Auto Scaling Group

The first step in creating an ASG is to create a *launch configuration*, which specifies how to configure each EC2 Instance in the ASG. The `aws_launch_configuration` resource uses almost exactly the same parameters as the `aws_instance` resource, so you can replace the latter with the former pretty easily:

```
resource "aws_launch_configuration" "example" {
  image_id        = "ami-40d28157"
  instance_type   = "t2.micro"
  security_groups = ["${aws_security_group.instance.id}"]
```

---

11 For a deeper look at how to build highly available and scalable systems on AWS, see: *http://bit.ly/2mpSXUZ*.

```
    user_data = <<-EOF
              #!/bin/bash
              echo "Hello, World" > index.html
              nohup busybox httpd -f -p "${var.server_port}" &
              EOF

  lifecycle {
    create_before_destroy = true
  }
}
```

The only new addition is the lifecycle parameter, which is required for using a launch configuration with an ASG. The lifecycle parameter is an example of a *meta-parameter*, or a parameter that exists on just about every resource in Terraform. You can add a lifecycle block to any resource to configure how that resource should be created, updated, or destroyed.

One of the available lifecycle settings is create_before_destroy, which, if set to true, tells Terraform to always create a replacement resource before destroying the original resource. For example, if you set create_before_destroy to true on an EC2 Instance, then whenever you make a change to that Instance, Terraform will first create a new EC2 Instance, wait for it to come up, and then remove the old EC2 Instance.

The catch with the create_before_destroy parameter is that if you set it to true on resource X, you also have to set it to true on every resource that X depends on (if you forget, you'll get errors about cyclical dependencies). In the case of the launch configuration, that means you need to set create_before_destroy to true on the security group:

```
resource "aws_security_group" "instance" {
  name = "terraform-example-instance"

  ingress {
    from_port   = "${var.server_port}"
    to_port     = "${var.server_port}"
    protocol    = "tcp"
    cidr_blocks = ["0.0.0.0/0"]
  }

  lifecycle {
    create_before_destroy = true
  }
}
```

Now you can create the ASG itself using the aws_autoscaling_group resource:

```
resource "aws_autoscaling_group" "example" {
  launch_configuration = "${aws_launch_configuration.example.id}"
```

```
    min_size = 2
    max_size = 10

    tag {
      key                 = "Name"
      value               = "terraform-asg-example"
      propagate_at_launch = true
    }
  }
}
```

This ASG will run between 2 and 10 EC2 Instances (defaulting to 2 for the initial launch), each tagged with the name "terraform-example". The ASG references the launch configuration you created earlier using Terraform's interpolation syntax.

To make this ASG work, you need to specify one more parameter: availabil ity_zones. This parameter tells the ASG into which availability zones (AZs) the EC2 Instances should be deployed. Each AZ represents an isolated AWS data center, so by deploying your Instances across multiple AZs, you ensure that your service can keep running even if some of the AZs have an outage. You could hard-code the list of AZs (e.g., set it to ["us-east-1a", "us-east-1b"]), but each AWS account has access to a slightly different set of AZs, so a better option is to use the aws_availabil ity_zones data source to fetch the AZs specific to your AWS account:

```
data "aws_availability_zones" "all" {}
```

A *data source* represents a piece of read-only information that is fetched from the provider (in this case, AWS) every time you run Terraform. Adding a data source to your Terraform configurations does not create anything new; it's just a way to query the provider's APIs for data. There are data sources to not only get the list of availability zones, but also AMI IDs, IP address ranges, and the current user's identity.

To use the data source, you reference it using the following syntax:

```
"${data.TYPE.NAME.ATTRIBUTE}"
```

For example, here is how you pass the names of the AZs from the aws_availabil ity_zones data source into the availability_zones parameter of the ASG:

```
resource "aws_autoscaling_group" "example" {
  launch_configuration = "${aws_launch_configuration.example.id}"
  availability_zones = ["${data.aws_availability_zones.all.names}"]

  min_size = 2
  max_size = 10

  tag {
    key                 = "Name"
    value               = "terraform-asg-example"
    propagate_at_launch = true
```

```
    }
}
```

Deploy a Load Balancer

At this point, you can deploy your ASG, but you'll have a small problem: you now have several different servers, each with its own IP addresses, but you typically want to give your end users only a single IP to hit. One way to solve this problem is to deploy a *load balancer* to distribute traffic across your servers and to give all your users the IP (actually, the DNS name) of the load balancer. Creating a load balancer that is highly available and scalable is a lot of work. Once again, you can let AWS take care of it for you, this time by using Amazon's *Elastic Load Balancer (ELB)* service, as shown in Figure 2-10.[12]

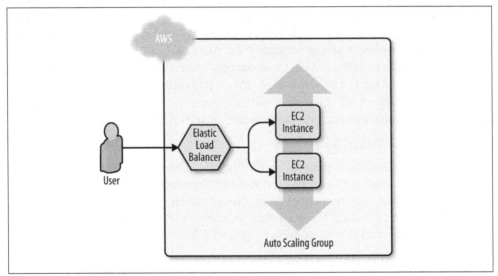

Figure 2-10. Use an Elastic Load Balancer to distribute traffic across the Auto Scaling Group

To create an ELB with Terraform, you use the `aws_elb` resource:

```
resource "aws_elb" "example" {
  name               = "terraform-asg-example"
  availability_zones = ["${data.aws_availability_zones.all.names}"]
}
```

---

12 Although all the examples in this book use the ELB, AWS has recently released a new service called the Application Load Balancer (ALB) (*http://amzn.to/2llkcee*) that may be a better choice for HTTP-based services.

This creates an ELB that will work across all of the AZs in your account. Of course, this definition doesn't do much until you tell the ELB how to route requests. To do that, you add one or more *listeners* that specify what port the ELB should listen on and what port it should route the request to:

```
resource "aws_elb" "example" {
  name                = "terraform-asg-example"
  availability_zones  = ["${data.aws_availability_zones.all.names}"]

  listener {
    lb_port           = 80
    lb_protocol       = "http"
    instance_port     = "${var.server_port}"
    instance_protocol = "http"
  }
}
```

This code tells the ELB to receive HTTP requests on port 80 (the default port for HTTP) and to route them to the port used by the Instances in the ASG. Note that, by default, ELBs don't allow any incoming or outgoing traffic (just like EC2 Instances), so you need to create a new security group that explicitly allows incoming requests on port 80:

```
resource "aws_security_group" "elb" {
  name = "terraform-example-elb"

  ingress {
    from_port   = 80
    to_port     = 80
    protocol    = "tcp"
    cidr_blocks = ["0.0.0.0/0"]
  }
}
```

And now you need to tell the ELB to use this security group by using the security_groups parameter:

```
resource "aws_elb" "example" {
  name                = "terraform-asg-example"
  availability_zones  = ["${data.aws_availability_zones.all.names}"]
  security_groups     = ["${aws_security_group.elb.id}"]

  listener {
    lb_port           = 80
    lb_protocol       = "http"
    instance_port     = "${var.server_port}"
    instance_protocol = "http"
  }
}
```

The ELB has one other trick up its sleeve: it can periodically check the health of your EC2 Instances and, if an Instance is unhealthy, it will automatically stop routing traffic to it. To configure a health check for the ELB, you add a health_check block. For example, here is a health_check block that sends an HTTP request every 30 seconds to the "/" URL of each of the EC2 Instances in the ASG and only considers an Instance healthy if it responds with a 200 OK:

```
resource "aws_elb" "example" {
  name               = "terraform-asg-example"
  availability_zones = ["${data.aws_availability_zones.all.names}"]
  security_groups    = ["${aws_security_group.elb.id}"]

  listener {
    lb_port           = 80
    lb_protocol       = "http"
    instance_port     = "${var.server_port}"
    instance_protocol = "http"
  }

  health_check {
    healthy_threshold   = 2
    unhealthy_threshold = 2
    timeout             = 3
    interval            = 30
    target              = "HTTP:${var.server_port}/"
  }
}
```

To allow these health check requests, you need to modify the ELB's security group to allow outbound requests:

```
resource "aws_security_group" "elb" {
  name = "terraform-example-elb"

  ingress {
    from_port   = 80
    to_port     = 80
    protocol    = "tcp"
    cidr_blocks = ["0.0.0.0/0"]
  }

  egress {
    from_port   = 0
    to_port     = 0
    protocol    = "-1"
    cidr_blocks = ["0.0.0.0/0"]
  }
}
```

How does the ELB know which EC2 Instances to send requests to? You can attach a static list of EC2 Instances to an ELB using the ELB's instances parameter, but with an ASG, Instances may launch or terminate at any time, so a static list won't work. Instead, you can go back to the aws_autoscaling_group resource and set its `load_balancers` parameter to tell the ASG to register each Instance in the ELB when that Instance is booting:

```
resource "aws_autoscaling_group" "example" {
  launch_configuration = "${aws_launch_configuration.example.id}"
  availability_zones = ["${data.aws_availability_zones.all.names}"]

  load_balancers    = ["${aws_elb.example.name}"]
  health_check_type = "ELB"

  min_size = 2
  max_size = 10

  tag {
    key                 = "Name"
    value               = "terraform-asg-example"
    propagate_at_launch = true
  }
}
```

Notice that the `health_check_type` is now `"ELB"`. This tells the ASG to use the ELB's health check to determine if an Instance is healthy or not and to automatically replace Instances if the ELB reports them as unhealthy.

One last thing to do before deploying the load balancer: replace the old `public_ip` output of the single EC2 Instance you had before with an output that shows the DNS name of the ELB:

```
output "elb_dns_name" {
  value = "${aws_elb.example.dns_name}"
}
```

Run the `plan` command to verify your changes. You should see that your original single EC2 Instance is being removed and in its place, Terraform will create a launch configuration, ASG, ELB, and a security group. If the plan looks good, run `apply`. When `apply` completes, you should see the `elb_dns_name` output:

```
Outputs:
elb_dns_name = terraform-asg-example-123.us-east-1.elb.amazonaws.com
```

Copy this URL down. It'll take a couple minutes for the Instances to boot and show up as healthy in the ELB. In the meantime, you can inspect what you've deployed. Open up the ASG section of the EC2 console (*https://console.aws.amazon.com/ec2/ autoscaling/home*), and you should see that the ASG has been created, as shown in Figure 2-11.

Figure 2-11. The Auto Scaling Group

If you switch over to the Instances tab, you'll see the two EC Instances launching, as shown in Figure 2-12.

Figure 2-12. The EC2 Instances in the ASG are launching

And finally, if you switch over to the Load Balancers tab, you'll see your ELB, as shown in Figure 2-13.

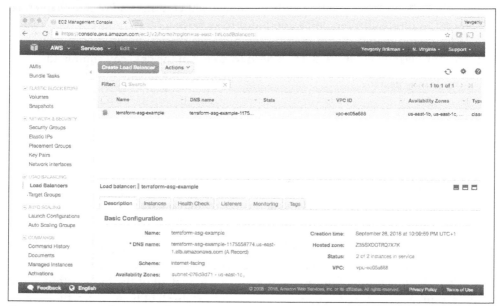

Figure 2-13. The Elastic Load Balancer

Wait for the "Status" indicator to say "2 of 2 instances in service." This typically takes 1 to 2 minutes. Once you see it, test the elb_dns_name output you copied earlier:

```
> curl http://<elb_dns_name>
Hello, World
```

Success! The ELB is routing traffic to your EC2 Instances. Each time you hit the URL, it'll pick a different Instance to handle the request. You now have a fully working cluster of web servers!

At this point, you can see how your cluster responds to firing up new Instances or shutting down old ones. For example, go to the Instances tab, and terminate one of the Instances by selecting its checkbox, selecting the "Actions" button at the top, and setting the "Instance State" to "Terminate." Continue to test the ELB URL and you should get a 200 OK for each request, even while terminating an Instance, as the ELB will automatically detect that the Instance is down and stop routing to it. Even more interestingly, a short time after the Instance shuts down, the ASG will detect that fewer than two Instances are running, and automatically launch a new one to replace it (self-healing!). You can also see how the ASG resizes itself by adding a desired_capacity parameter to your Terraform code and rerunning apply.

Cleanup

When you're done experimenting with Terraform, either at the end of this chapter, or at the end of future chapters, it's a good idea to remove all the resources you created so AWS doesn't charge you for them. Since Terraform keeps track of what resources you created, cleanup is simple. All you need to do is run the `destroy` command:

```
> terraform destroy

Do you really want to destroy?
  Terraform will delete all your managed infrastructure.
  There is no undo. Only 'yes' will be accepted to confirm.

Enter a value:
```

Once you type in "yes" and hit Enter, Terraform will build the dependency graph and delete all the resources in the right order, using as much parallelism as possible. In a minute or two, your AWS account should be clean again.

Note that later in the book, you will continue to evolve this example, so don't delete the Terraform code! However, feel free to run `destroy` on the actual deployed resources. After all, the beauty of infrastructure as code is that all of the information about those resources is captured in code, so you can re-create all of them at any time with a single command: `terraform apply`. In fact, you may want to commit your latest changes to Git so you can keep track of the history of your infrastructure.

Conclusion

You now have a basic grasp of how to use Terraform. The declarative language makes it easy to describe exactly the infrastructure you want to create. The `plan` command allows you to verify your changes and catch bugs before deploying them. Variables, interpolation, and dependencies allow you to remove duplication from your code and make it highly configurable.

However, you've only scratched the surface. In Chapter 3, you'll learn how Terraform keeps track of what infrastructure it has already created, and the profound impact that has on how you should structure your Terraform code. In Chapter 4, you'll see how to create reusable infrastructure with Terraform modules.

## CHAPTER 3

How to Manage Terraform State

In Chapter 2, as you were using Terraform to create and update resources, you may have noticed that every time you ran `terraform plan` or `terraform apply`, Terraform was able to find the resources it created previously and update them accordingly. But how did Terraform know which resources it was supposed to manage? You could have all sorts of infrastructure in your AWS account, deployed through a variety of mechanisms (some manually, some via Terraform, some via the CLI), so how does Terraform know which infrastructure it's responsible for?

In this chapter, you're going to see how Terraform tracks the state of your infrastructure and the impact that has on file layout, isolation, and locking in a Terraform project. Here are the key topics I'll go over:

- What is Terraform state?
- Shared storage for state files
- Locking state files
- Isolating state files
- File layout
- Read-only state

Example Code

As a reminder, all of the code examples in the book can be found at the following URL: *https://github.com/brikis98/terraform-up-and-running-code*.

What Is Terraform State?

Every time you run Terraform, it records information about what infrastructure it created in a *Terraform state file*. By default, when you run Terraform in the folder */foo/bar*, Terraform creates the file */foo/bar/terraform.tfstate*. This file contains a custom JSON format that records a mapping from the Terraform resources in your configuration files to the representation of those resources in the real world. For example, let's say your Terraform configuration contained the following:

```
resource "aws_instance" "example" {
  ami           = "ami-40d28157"
  instance_type = "t2.micro"
}
```

After running `terraform apply`, here is a small snippet of the contents of the *terraform.tfstate* file:

```
{
  "aws_instance.example": {
    "type": "aws_instance",
    "primary": {
      "id": "i-66ba8957",
      "attributes": {
        "ami": "ami-40d28157",
        "availability_zone": "us-east-1d",
        "id": "i-66ba8957",
        "instance_state": "running",
        "instance_type": "t2.micro",
        "network_interface_id": "eni-7c4fcf6e",
        "private_dns": "ip-172-31-53-99.ec2.internal",
        "private_ip": "172.31.53.99",
        "public_dns": "ec2-54-159-88-79.compute-1.amazonaws.com",
        "public_ip": "54.159.88.79",
        "subnet_id": "subnet-3b29db10"
      }
    }
  }
}
```

Using this simple JSON format, Terraform knows that `aws_instance.example` corresponds to an EC2 Instance in your AWS account with ID `i-66ba8957`. Every time you run Terraform, it can fetch the latest status of this EC2 Instance from AWS and compare that to what's in your Terraform configurations to determine what changes need to be applied.

The State File Is a Private API

The state file format is a private API that changes with every release and is meant only for internal use within Terraform. You should never edit the Terraform state files by hand or write code that reads them directly.

If for some reason you need to manipulate the state file—which should be a relatively rare occurrence—use the `terraform import` command (you'll see an example of this in Chapter 5) or the `terraform state` command (this is only for advanced use cases).

If you're using Terraform for a personal project, storing state in a local *terraform.tfstate* file works just fine. But if you want to use Terraform as a team on a real product, you run into several problems:

Shared storage for state files

To be able to use Terraform to update your infrastructure, each of your team members needs access to the same Terraform state files. That means you need to store those files in a shared location.

Locking state files

As soon as data is shared, you run into a new problem: locking. Without locking, if two team members are running Terraform at the same time, you may run into race conditions as multiple Terraform processes make concurrent updates to the state files, leading to conflicts, data loss, and state file corruption.

Isolating state files

When making changes to your infrastructure, it's a best practice to isolate different environments. For example, when making a change in a testing or staging environment, you want to be sure that there is no way you can accidentally break production. But how can you isolate your changes if all of your infrastructure is defined in the same Terraform state file?

In the following sections, I'll dive into each of these problems and show you how to solve them.

Shared Storage for State Files

The most common technique for allowing multiple team members to access a common set of files is to put them in version control (e.g., Git). With Terraform state, this is a *bad idea* for two reasons:

Manual error

It's too easy to forget to pull down the latest changes from version control before running Terraform or to push your latest changes to version control after running Terraform. It's just a matter of time before someone on your team runs Terraform with out-of-date state files and as a result, accidentally rolls back or duplicates previous deployments.

Secrets

All data in Terraform state files is stored in plain text. This is a problem because certain Terraform resources need to store sensitive data. For example, if you use the `aws_db_instance` resource to create a database, Terraform will store the username and password for the database in a state file in plain text. Storing plain-text secrets *anywhere* is a bad idea, including version control. As of November, 2016, this is an open issue (*https://github.com/hashicorp/terraform/issues/516*) in the Terraform community, although there are some reasonable workarounds, as I will discuss shortly.

Instead of using version control, the best way to manage shared storage for state files is to use Terraform's built-in support for *Remote State Storage*. Using the `terraform remote config` command, you can configure Terraform to fetch and store state data from a remote store every time it runs. Several remote stores are supported, such as Amazon S3, Azure Storage, HashiCorp Consul, and HashiCorp's Terraform Pro and Terraform Enterprise.

I typically recommend Amazon S3 (Simple Storage Service), which is Amazon's managed file store, for the following reasons:

- It's a managed service, so you don't have to deploy and manage extra infrastructure to use it.

- It's designed for 99.999999999% durability and 99.99% availability, which effectively means it'll never lose your data or go down.[1]

- It supports encryption, which reduces worries about storing sensitive data in state files. Anyone on your team who has access to that S3 bucket will be able to see the state files in an unencrypted form, so this is still a partial solution, but at least the data will be encrypted at rest (S3 supports server-side encryption using AES-256) and in transit (Terraform uses SSL to read and write data in S3).

- It supports *versioning*, so every revision of your state file is stored, and you can always roll back to an older version if something goes wrong.

- It's inexpensive, with most Terraform usage easily fitting into the free tier.[2]

---

[1] Learn more about S3's guarantees here: *https://aws.amazon.com/s3/details/#durability*.

[2] See pricing information for S3 here: *https://aws.amazon.com/s3/pricing/*.

S3 and Large, Distributed Teams

S3 is an eventually consistent file store, which means changes can take a few seconds to propagate. If you have a large, geographically distributed team that makes frequent changes to the same Terraform state, there is a very small chance you will end up with stale state. For these sorts of use cases, you may want to use an alternate remote state store, such as Terraform Pro or Terraform Enterprise.

To enable remote state storage with S3, the first step is to create an S3 bucket. Create a *main.tf* file in a new folder (it should be a different folder from where you store the configurations from Chapter 2) and at the top of the file, specify AWS as the provider:

```
provider "aws" {
  region = "us-east-1"
}
```

Next, create an S3 bucket by using the `aws_s3_bucket` resource:

```
resource "aws_s3_bucket" "terraform_state" {
  bucket = "terraform-up-and-running-state"

  versioning {
    enabled = true
  }

  lifecycle {
    prevent_destroy = true
  }
}
```

This code sets three parameters:

bucket

> This is the name of the S3 bucket. Note that it must be *globally* unique. Therefore, you will have to change the bucket parameter from "terraform-up-and-running-state" (which I already created) to your own name.[3] Make sure to remember this name and take note of what AWS region you're using, as you'll need both pieces of information again a little later on.

versioning

> This block enables versioning on the S3 bucket, so that every update to a file in the bucket actually creates a new version of that file. This allows you to see older versions of the file and revert to those older versions at any time.

---

3 See here for more information on S3 bucket names: *http://bit.ly/2b1s7eh*.

prevent_destroy

> prevent_destroy is the second lifecycle setting you've seen (the first was cre ate_before_destroy). When you set prevent_destroy to true on a resource, any attempt to delete that resource (e.g., by running terraform destroy) will cause Terraform to exit with an error. This is a good way to prevent accidental deletion of an important resource, such as this S3 bucket, which will store all of your Terraform state. Of course, if you really mean to delete it, you can just comment that setting out.

Run terraform plan, and if everything looks OK, create the bucket by running ter raform apply. After this completes, you will have an S3 bucket, but your Terraform state is still stored locally. To configure Terraform to store the state in your S3 bucket (with encryption), run the following command, filling in your own values where specified:

```
> terraform remote config \
    -backend=s3 \
    -backend-config="bucket=(YOUR_BUCKET_NAME)" \
    -backend-config="key=global/s3/terraform.tfstate" \
    -backend-config="region=us-east-1" \
    -backend-config="encrypt=true"

Remote configuration updated
Remote state configured and pulled.
```

After running this command, your Terraform state will be stored in the S3 bucket. You can check this by heading over to the S3 console (*https:// console.aws.amazon.com/s3/*) in your browser and clicking your bucket. You should see something similar to Figure 3-1.

Figure 3-1. Terraform state file stored in S3

With remote state enabled, Terraform will automatically pull the latest state from this S3 bucket before running a command, and automatically push the latest state to the S3 bucket after running a command. To see this in action, add the following output variable:

```
output "s3_bucket_arn" {
  value = "${aws_s3_bucket.terraform_state.arn}"
}
```

This variable will print out the Amazon Resource Name (ARN) of your S3 bucket. Run terraform apply to see it:

```
> terraform apply

aws_s3_bucket.terraform_state: Refreshing state...
(ID: terraform-up-and-running-state)

Apply complete! Resources: 0 added, 0 changed, 0 destroyed.

Outputs:

s3_bucket_arn = arn:aws:s3:::terraform-up-and-running-state
```

Now, head over to the S3 console (*https://console.aws.amazon.com/s3/*) again, refresh the page, and click the gray "Show" button next to "Versions." You should now see several versions of your *terraform.tfstate* file in the S3 bucket, as shown in Figure 3-2.

Figure 3-2. Multiple versions of the Terraform state file in S3

This means that Terraform is automatically pushing and pulling state data to and from S3 and S3 is storing every revision of the state file, which can be useful for debugging and rolling back to older versions if something goes wrong.

Locking State Files

Enabling remote state solves the problem of how you share state files with your teammates, but it creates two new problems:

1. Each developer on your team needs to remember to run the `terraform remote config` command for every Terraform project. It's easy to mess up or forget to run this long command.

2. While Terraform remote state storage ensures your state is stored in a shared location, it does *not* provide locking for that shared location. Therefore, race conditions are still possible if two developers are using Terraform at the same time on the same state files.

Future versions of Terraform may solve both of these problems by introducing the concept of "backends," (*https://github.com/hashicorp/terraform/pull/11286*) but in the meantime, you can pick from one of these other solutions:

Terraform Pro or Terraform Enterprise
  While Terraform itself is open source, HashiCorp, the company that created Terraform, offers paid options called Terraform Pro and Terraform Enterprise (*https://www.hashicorp.com/terraform.html*), each of which supports locking for state files.

Build server
  To remove the need for locking entirely, you can enforce a rule in your team that no one can run Terraform locally to modify a shared environment (e.g., staging, production). Instead, all the changes must be applied automatically by a *build server*, such as Jenkins or CircleCI, which you can configure to never apply more than one change concurrently. Using a build server to automate deployments is a good idea regardless of the locking strategy you use, as it allows you to catch bugs and enforce compliance rules by running automated tests before applying any change. I'll come back to build servers in Chapter 6.

Terragrunt
  Terragrunt is a thin, open source wrapper for Terraform that configures remote state automatically and provides locking by using Amazon DynamoDB (*https://aws.amazon.com/dynamodb/*). DynamoDB is part of the AWS free tier, so using it for locking should be free for most teams.

The easiest solution to start with is Terragrunt, since it's free and does not require setting up any extra infrastructure. To try it out, head over to the Terragrunt GitHub page (*https://github.com/gruntwork-io/terragrunt*) and follow the instructions in the Readme to install the appropriate Terragrunt binary for your operating system. Next, create a file called *.terragrunt* in the same folder as the Terraform configuration for your S3 bucket, and put the following code in it, filling in your own values where specified:

```
# Configure Terragrunt to use DynamoDB for locking
lock = {
  backend = "dynamodb"

  config {
    state_file_id = "global/s3"
  }
}

# Configure Terragrunt to automatically store tfstate files in S3
remote_state = {
  backend = "s3"

  config {
    encrypt = "true"
    bucket  = "(YOUR_BUCKET_NAME)"
    key     = "global/s3/terraform.tfstate"
    region  = "us-east-1"
  }
}
```

The *.terragrunt* file uses the same language as Terraform, HCL. The first part of the configuration tells Terragrunt to use DynamoDB for locking. The `state_file_id` should be unique for each set of Terraform configurations, so they each have their own lock. The second part of the configuration tells Terragrunt to use an S3 bucket for remote state storage using the exact same settings as the `terraform remote config` command you ran earlier.

Once you check this *.terragrunt* file into source control, everyone on your team can use Terragrunt to run all the standard Terraform commands:

```
> terragrunt plan
> terragrunt apply
> terragrunt output
> terragrunt destroy
```

Terragrunt forwards almost all commands, arguments, and options directly to Terraform, using whatever version of Terraform you already have installed. However, before running Terraform, Terragrunt will ensure your remote state is configured according to the settings in the *.terragrunt* file. Moreover, for any commands that could change your Terraform state (e.g., `apply` and `destroy`), Terragrunt will acquire and release a lock using DynamoDB.

Here's what it looks like in action:

```
> terragrunt apply

[terragrunt] Configuring remote state for the s3 backend
[terragrunt] Running command: terraform remote config
[terragrunt] Attempting to acquire lock in DynamoDB
[terragrunt] Attempting to create lock item table terragrunt_locks
[terragrunt] Lock acquired!
[terragrunt] Running command: terraform apply

terraform apply

aws_instance.example: Creating...
  ami:           "" => "ami-0d729a60"
  instance_type: "" => "t2.micro"

(...)

Apply complete! Resources: 1 added, 0 changed, 0 destroyed.

[terragrunt] Attempting to release lock
[terragrunt] Lock released!
```

In this output, you can see that Terragrunt automatically configured remote state as declared in the *.terragrunt* file, acquired a lock from DynamoDB, ran `terraform apply`, and then released the lock. If anyone else already had the lock, Terragrunt would have waited until the lock was released to prevent race conditions. Future developers need only check out the repository containing this folder and run `terragrunt apply` to achieve an identical result!

Isolating State Files

With remote state storage and locking, collaboration is no longer a problem. However, there is still one more problem remaining: isolation. When you first start using Terraform, you may be tempted to define all of your infrastructure in a single Terraform file or a set of Terraform files in one folder. The problem with this approach is that all of your Terraform state is now stored in a single file, too, and a mistake anywhere could break everything.

For example, while trying to deploy a new version of your app in staging, you might break the app in production. Or worse yet, you might corrupt your entire state file, either because you didn't use locking, or due to a rare Terraform bug, and now all of your infrastructure in all environments is broken.[4]

The whole point of having separate environments is that they are isolated from each other, so if you are managing all the environments from a single set of Terraform configurations, you are breaking that isolation. Just as a ship has bulkheads that act as barriers to prevent a leak in one part of the ship from immediately flooding all the others, you should have "bulkheads" built into your Terraform design, as shown in Figure 3-3.

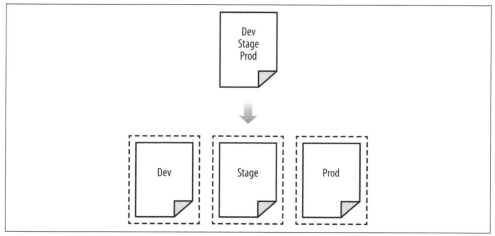

Figure 3-3. Instead of defining all your environments in a single set of Terraform configurations (top), you want to define each environment in a separate set of configurations (bottom), so a problem in one environment is completely isolated from the others.

The way to do that is to put the Terraform configuration files for each environment into a separate folder. For example, all the configurations for the staging environment can be in a folder called *stage* and all the configurations for the production environment can be in a folder called *prod*. That way, Terraform will use a separate state file for each environment, which makes it significantly less likely that a screw up in one environment can have any impact on another.

In fact, you may want to take the isolation concept beyond environments and down to the "component" level, where a component is a coherent set of resources that you typically deploy together. For example, once you've set up the basic network topology for your infrastructure—in AWS lingo, your Virtual Private Cloud (VPC) and all the associated subnets, routing rules, VPNs, and network ACLs—you will probably only change it once every few months. On the other hand, you may deploy a new version

---

4 For a colorful example of what happens when you don't isolate Terraform state, see: *http://bit.ly/2lTsewM*.

of a web server multiple times per day. If you manage the infrastructure for both the VPC component and the web server component in the same set of Terraform configurations, you are unnecessarily putting your entire network topology at risk of breakage multiple times per day.

Therefore, I recommend using separate Terraform folders (and therefore separate state files) for each environment (staging, production, etc.) and each component (vpc, services, databases). To see what this looks like in practice, let's go through the recommended file layout for Terraform projects.

File Layout

Figure 3-4 shows the file layout for my typical Terraform project.

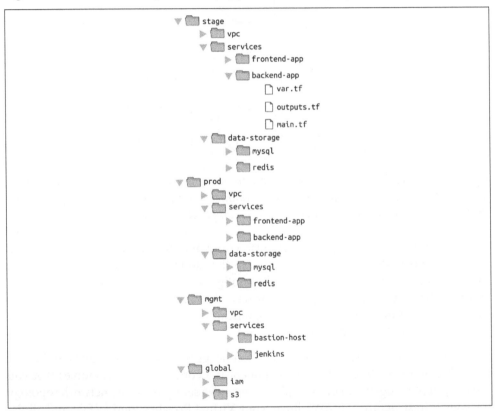

Figure 3-4. Typical file layout for a Terraform project

At the top level, there are separate folders for each "environment." The exact environments differ for every project, but the typical ones are:

stage

An environment for nonproduction workloads (i.e., testing).

prod

An environment for production workloads (i.e., user-facing apps).

mgmt

An environment for DevOps tooling (e.g., bastion host, Jenkins).

global

A place to put resources that are used across all environments (e.g., S3, IAM).

Within each environment, there are separate folders for each "component." The components differ for every project, but the typical ones are:

vpc

The network topology for this environment.

services

The apps or microservices to run in this environment, such as a Ruby on Rails frontend or a Scala backend. Each app could even live in its own folder to isolate it from all the other apps.

data-storage

The data stores to run in this environment, such as MySQL or Redis. Each data store could even live in its own folder to isolate it from all other data stores.

Within each component, there are the actual Terraform configuration files, which are organized according to the following naming conventions:

vars.tf

Input variables.

outputs.tf

Output variables.

main.tf

The actual resources.

When you run Terraform, it simply looks for files in the current directory with the *.tf* extension, so you can use whatever filenames you want. Using a consistent convention like this makes your code easier to browse, since you always know where to look to find a variable, output, or resource. If your Terraform configurations are becoming massive, it's OK to break out certain functionality into separate files (e.g., *iam.tf, s3.tf, database.tf*), but that may also be a sign that you should break your code into smaller modules instead, a topic I'll dive into in Chapter 4.

Avoiding Copy/Paste

The file layout described in this section has a lot of duplication. For example, the same frontend-app and backend-app live in both the *stage* and *prod* folders. Don't worry, you won't need to copy/paste all of that code! In Chapter 4, you'll see how to use Terraform modules to keep all of this code DRY.

Let's take the web server cluster code you wrote in Chapter 2, plus the S3 bucket code you wrote in this chapter, and rearrange it using the folder structure in Figure 3-5.

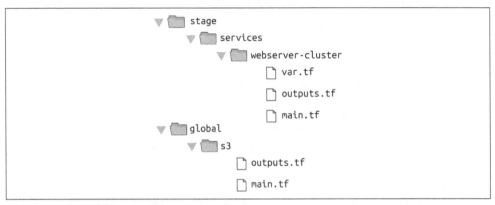

Figure 3-5. File layout for the web server cluster code

The S3 bucket you created in this chapter should be moved into the *global/s3* folder. Note that you'll need to move the s3_bucket_arn output variable to *outputs.tf*. If you configured remote state storage, make sure you don't miss the (hidden) *.terraform* folder when copying files to the new location.

The web server cluster you created in Chapter 2 should be moved into *stage/services/webserver-cluster* (think of this as the "testing" or "staging" version of that web server cluster; you'll add a "production" version in the next chapter). Again, make sure to copy over the *.terraform* folder, move input variables into *vars.tf*, and output variables into *outputs.tf*.

You should also configure remote state storage in S3 for the web server cluster (e.g., by running the terraform remote config command). Set the S3 key to the same path as the web server Terraform code: *state/services/webserver-cluster/terraform.tfstate*. This gives you a 1:1 mapping between the layout of your Terraform code in version control and your Terraform state files in S3, so it's obvious how the two are connected.

This file layout makes it easy to browse the code and understand exactly what components are deployed in each environment. It also provides a good amount of isolation between environments and between components within an environment, ensuring that if something goes wrong, the damage is contained as much as possible to just one small part of your entire infrastructure.

Of course, this very same property is, in some ways, a drawback, too: splitting components into separate folders prevents you from breaking multiple components in one command, but it also prevents you from creating all the components in one command. If all of the components for a single environment were defined in a single Terraform configuration, you could spin up an entire environment with a single call to `terraform apply`. But if all the components are in separate folders, then you need to run `terraform apply` separately in each one (note that if you're using Terragrunt, you can automate this process using the `spin-up` command[5]).

There is another problem with this file layout: it makes it harder to use resource dependencies. If your app code was defined in the same Terraform configuration files as the database code, then that app could directly access attributes of the database (e.g., the database address and port) using Terraform's interpolation syntax (e.g., $ {aws_db_instance.foo.address}). But if the app code and database code live in different folders, as I've recommended, you can no longer do that. Fortunately, Terraform offers a solution: read-only state.

Read-Only State

In Chapter 2, you used data sources to fetch read-only information from AWS, such as the `aws_availability_zones` data source, which returns a list of availability zones in the current region. There is another data source that is particularly useful when working with state: `terraform_remote_state`. You can use this data source to fetch the Terraform state file stored by another set of Terraform configurations in a completely read-only manner.

Let's go through an example. Imagine that your web server cluster needs to talk to a MySQL database. Running a database that is scalable, secure, durable, and highly available is a lot of work. Once again, you can let AWS take care of it for you, this time by using the *Relational Database Service (RDS)*, as shown in Figure 3-6. RDS supports a variety of databases, including MySQL, PostgreSQL, SQL Server, and Oracle.

---

5 For more information, see Terragrunt's documentation (*https://github.com/gruntwork-io/terragrunt*).

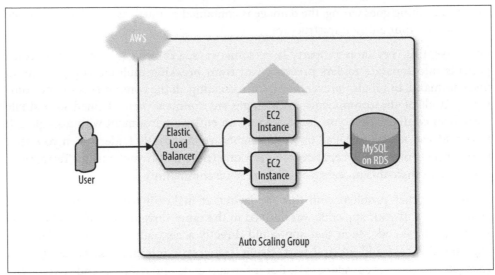

Figure 3-6. The web server cluster talks to MySQL, which is deployed on top of Amazon's Relational Database Service

You may not want to define the MySQL database in the same set of configuration files as the web server cluster, as you'll be deploying updates to the web server cluster far more frequently and don't want to risk accidentally breaking the database each time you do so. Therefore, your first step should be to create a new folder at *stage/data-stores/mysql* and create the basic Terraform files (*main.tf, vars.tf, outputs.tf*) within it, as shown in Figure 3-7.

Next, create the database resources in *stage/data-stores/mysql/main.tf*:

```
provider "aws" {
  region = "us-east-1"
}

resource "aws_db_instance" "example" {
  engine            = "mysql"
  allocated_storage = 10
  instance_class    = "db.t2.micro"
  name              = "example_database"
  username          = "admin"
  password          = "${var.db_password}"
}
```

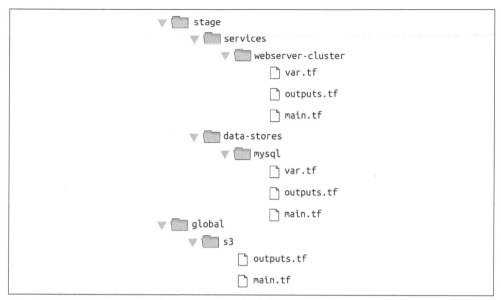

Figure 3-7. Create the database code in the stage/data-stores folder

At the top of the file, you see the typical `provider` resource, but just below that is a new resource: `aws_db_instance`. This resource creates a database in RDS. The settings in this code configure RDS to run MySQL with 10GB of storage on a `db.t2.micro` instance, which has 1 virtual CPU, 1GB of memory, and is part of the AWS free tier. Notice that in this code, the `password` parameter is set to the `var.db_password` input variable, which you should declare in *stage/data-stores/mysql/vars.tf*:

```
variable "db_password" {
  description = "The password for the database"
}
```

Note that this variable does not have a `default`. This is intentional. You should not store your database password or any sensitive information in plain text. Instead, you should store all secrets using a password manager that will encrypt your sensitive data (e.g., 1Password, LastPass, OS X Keychain) and expose those secrets to Terraform via environment variables. For each input variable `foo` defined in your Terraform configurations, you can provide Terraform the value of this variable using the environment variable `TF_VAR_foo`. For the `var.db_password` input variable, here is how you can set the `TF_VAR_db_password` environment variable on Linux/Unix/OS X systems:

```
> export TF_VAR_db_password="(YOUR_DB_PASSWORD)"
```

Next, configure remote state storage so that the database stores all of its state in S3 (e.g., by running the `terraform remote config` command) and set the S3 key to *stage/data-stores/mysql/terraform.tfstate*. As a reminder, Terraform stores all variables in its state files in plain text, including the database password, so make sure to enable encryption when configuring remote state.

Run `terraform plan`, and if the plan looks good, run `terraform apply` to create the database. Note that RDS can take as long as 10 minutes to provision even a small database, so be patient!

Now that you have a database, how do you provide its address and port to your web server cluster? The first step is to add two output variables to *stage/data-stores/mysql/outputs.tf*:

```
output "address" {
  value = "${aws_db_instance.example.address}"
}

output "port" {
  value = "${aws_db_instance.example.port}"
}
```

Run `terraform apply` one more time and you should see the outputs in the terminal:

```
> terraform apply

(...)

Apply complete! Resources: 0 added, 0 changed, 0 destroyed.

Outputs:

address = tf-2016111123.cowu6mts6srx.us-east-1.rds.amazonaws.com
port = 3306
```

These outputs are now also stored in the remote state for the database, which is in your S3 bucket at the path *stage/data-stores/mysql/terraform.tfstate*. You can get the web server cluster code to read the data from this state file by adding the `terraform_remote_state` data source in *stage/services/webserver-cluster/main.tf*:

```
data "terraform_remote_state" "db" {
  backend = "s3"

  config {
    bucket = "(YOUR_BUCKET_NAME)"
    key    = "stage/data-stores/mysql/terraform.tfstate"
    region = "us-east-1"
  }
}
```

This `terraform_remote_state` data source configures the web server cluster code to read the state file from the same S3 bucket and folder where the database stores its state, as shown in Figure 3-8.

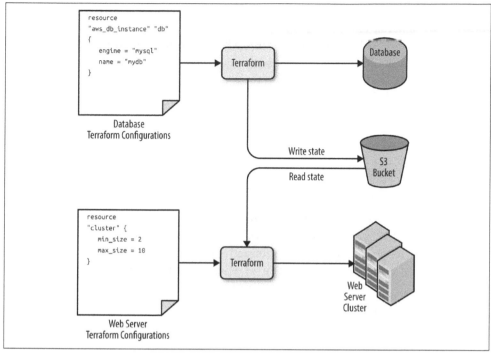

Figure 3-8. The database writes its state to an S3 bucket (top) and the web server cluster reads that state from the same bucket (bottom)

It's important to understand that, like all Terraform data sources, the data returned by terraform_remote_state is read-only. Nothing you do in your web server cluster Terraform code can modify that state, so you can pull in the database's state data with no risk of causing any problems in the database itself.

All the database's output variables are stored in the state file and you can read them from the terraform_remote_state data source using interpolation syntax:

```
"${data.terraform_remote_state.NAME.ATTRIBUTE}"
```

For example, here is how you can update the User Data of the web server cluster instances to pull the database address and port out of the terraform_remote_state data source and expose that information in the HTTP response:

```
user_data = <<EOF
#!/bin/bash
echo "Hello, World" >> index.html
echo "${data.terraform_remote_state.db.address}" >> index.html
echo "${data.terraform_remote_state.db.port}" >> index.html
nohup busybox httpd -f -p "${var.server_port}" &
EOF
```

As the User Data script is getting longer, defining it inline is getting messier and messier. In general, embedding one programming language (Bash) inside another (Terraform) makes it harder to maintain each one, so it's a good idea to externalize the Bash script. To do that, you can use the `file` interpolation function and the `template_file` data source. Let's talk about these one at a time.

An *interpolation function* is a function you can use within Terraform's interpolation syntax:

```
"${some_function(...)}"
```

For example, consider the `format` interpolation function:

```
"${format(FMT, ARGS, ...)}"
```

This function formats the arguments in ARGS according to the `sprintf` syntax in the string FMT.[6] A great way to experiment with interpolation functions is to run the `terraform console` command to get an interactive console where you can try out different Terraform syntax, query the state of your infrastructure, and see the results instantly:

```
terraform console

> format("%.3f", 3.14159265359)
3.142
```

Note that the Terraform console is read-only, so you don't have to worry about accidentally changing infrastructure or state!

There are a number of other built-in functions that can be used to manipulate strings, numbers, lists, and maps.[7] One of them is the `file` interpolation function:

```
"${file(PATH)}"
```

This function reads the file at PATH and returns its contents as a string. For example, you could put your User Data script into *stage/services/webserver-cluster/user-data.sh* and load its contents into the `user_data` parameter of the `aws_launch_configuration` resource as follows:

```
user_data = "${file("user-data.sh")}"
```

The catch is that the User Data script for the web server cluster needs some dynamic data from Terraform, including the server port, database address, and database port. When the User Data script was embedded in the Terraform code, you used interpola-

---

6 You can find documentation for the `sprintf` syntax here: *https://golang.org/pkg/fmt/*.

7 You can find the full list of interpolation functions here: *https://www.terraform.io/docs/configuration/interpolation.html*.

---

tion syntax to fill in these values. This does not work with the `file` interpolation function. However, it does work if you use a `template_file` data source.

The `template_file` data source has two parameters: the `template` parameter, which is a string, and the `vars` parameter, which is a map of variables. It has one output attribute called `rendered`, which is the result of rendering `template`, including any interpolation syntax in `template`, with the variables available in `vars`. To see this in action, add the following `template_file` data source to *stage/services/webserver-cluster/main.tf*:

```
data "template_file" "user_data" {
  template = "${file("user-data.sh")}"

  vars {
    server_port = "${var.server_port}"
    db_address  = "${data.terraform_remote_state.db.address}"
    db_port     = "${data.terraform_remote_state.db.port}"
  }
}
```

You can see that this code sets the `template` parameter to the contents of the *user-data.sh* script and the `vars` parameter to the three variables the User Data script needs: the server port, database address, and database port. To use these variables, here's what the *stage/services/webserver-cluster/user-data.sh* script should look like:

```
#!/bin/bash

cat > index.html <<EOF
<h1>Hello, World</h1>
<p>DB address: ${db_address}</p>
<p>DB port: ${db_port}</p>
EOF

nohup busybox httpd -f -p "${server_port}" &
```

Note that this Bash script has a few changes from the original:

- It looks up variables using Terraform's standard interpolation syntax, but the only available variables are the ones in the `vars` map of the `template_file` data source. Note that you don't need any prefix to access those variables: e.g., you should use ${server_port} and not ${var.server_port}.

- The script now includes some HTML syntax (e.g., <h1>) to make the output a bit more readable in a web browser.

A Note on Externalized Files

One of the benefits of extracting the User Data script into its own file is that you can write unit tests for it. The test code can even fill in the interpolated variables by using environment variables, since the Bash syntax for looking up environment variables is the same as Terraform's interpolation syntax. For example, you could write an automated test for *user-data.sh* along the following lines:

```
export db_address=12.34.56.78
export db_port=5555
export server_port=8888

./user-data.sh

output=$(curl "http://localhost:$server_port")

if [[ $output == *"Hello, World"* ]]; then
  echo "Success! Got expected text from server."
else
  echo "Error. Did not get back expected text 'Hello, World'."
fi
```

The final step is to update the user_data parameter of the aws_launch_configura
tion resource to point to the rendered output attribute of the template_file data source:

```
resource "aws_launch_configuration" "example" {
  image_id        = "ami-40d28157"
  instance_type   = "t2.micro"
  security_groups = ["${aws_security_group.instance.id}"]
  user_data       = "${data.template_file.user_data.rendered}"

  lifecycle {
    create_before_destroy = true
  }
}
```

Ah, that's much cleaner than writing Bash scripts inline!

If you deploy this cluster using terraform apply, wait for the Instances to register in the ELB, and open the ELB URL in a web browser, you'll see something similar to Figure 3-9.

Yay, your web server cluster can now programmatically access the database address and port via Terraform! If you were using a real web framework (e.g., Ruby on Rails), you could set the address and port as environment variables or write them to a config file so they could be used by your database library (e.g., ActiveRecord) to talk to the database.

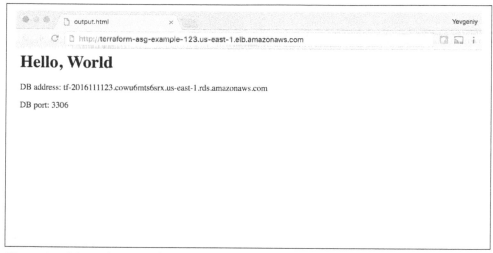

Figure 3-9. The web server cluster can programmatically access the database address and port

Conclusion

The reason you need to put so much thought into isolation, locking, and state is that infrastructure as code (IAC) has different trade-offs than normal coding. When you're writing code for a typical app, most bugs are relatively minor and only break a small part of a single app. When you're writing code that controls your infrastructure, bugs tend to be more severe, as they can break all of your apps—and all of your data stores and your entire network topology and just about everything else. Therefore, I recommend including more "safety mechanisms" when working on IAC than with typical code.[8]

A common concern of using the recommended file layout is that it leads to code duplication. If you want to run the web server cluster in both staging and production, how do you avoid having to copy and paste a lot of code between *stage/services/webserver-cluster* and *prod/services/webserver-cluster*? The answer is that you need to use Terraform modules, which are the main topic of Chapter 4.

---

8 For more information on software safety mechanisms, see *http://www.ybrikman.com/writing/2016/02/14/agility-requires-safety/*.

## CHAPTER 4

How to Create Reusable Infrastructure with Terraform Modules

At the end of Chapter 3, you had deployed the architecture shown in Figure 4-1.

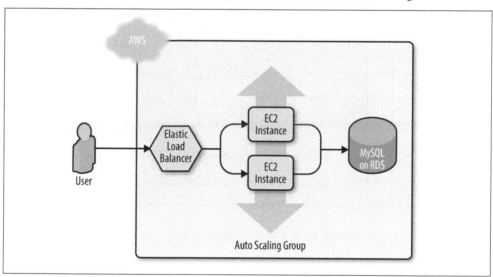

Figure 4-1. A load balancer, web server cluster, and database

This works great as a staging environment, but what about the production environment? You don't want your users accessing the same environment your employees use for testing, and it's too risky testing in production, so you typically need two environments, staging and production, as shown in Figure 4-2. Ideally, the two environments are nearly identical, though you may run slightly fewer/smaller servers in staging to save money.

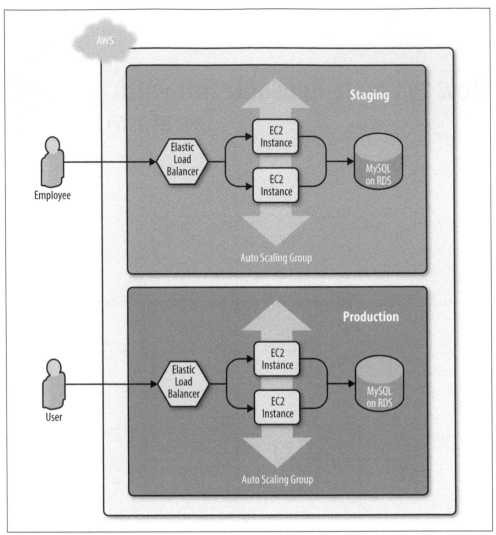

Figure 4-2. Two environments, each with its own load balancer, web server cluster, and database

With just a staging environment, the file layout for your Terraform code looked something like Figure 4-3.

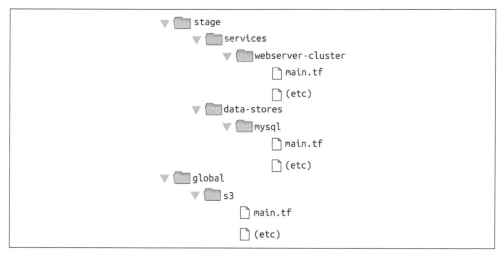

Figure 4-3. File layout with only a staging environment

If you were to add a production environment, you'd end up with the file layout in Figure 4-4.

How do you avoid duplication between the staging and production environments? How do you avoid having to copy and paste all the code in *stage/services/webserver-cluster* into *prod/services/webserver-cluster* and all the code in *stage/data-stores/mysql* into *prod/data-stores/mysql*?

In a general-purpose programming language (e.g., Ruby, Python, Java), if you had the same code copied and pasted in several places, you could put that code inside of a function and reuse that function in multiple places throughout your code:

```
def example_function()
  puts "Hello, World"
end

# Other places in your code
example_function()
```

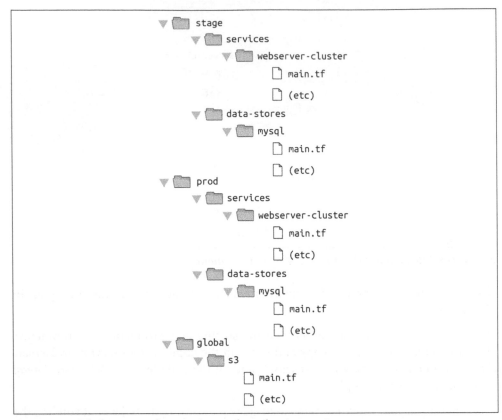

Figure 4-4. File layout with a staging and production environment

With Terraform, you can put your code inside of a *Terraform module* and reuse that module in multiple places throughout your code. The *stage/services/webserver-cluster* and *prod/services/webserver-cluster* configurations can both reuse code from the same module without the need to copy and paste (see Figure 4-5).

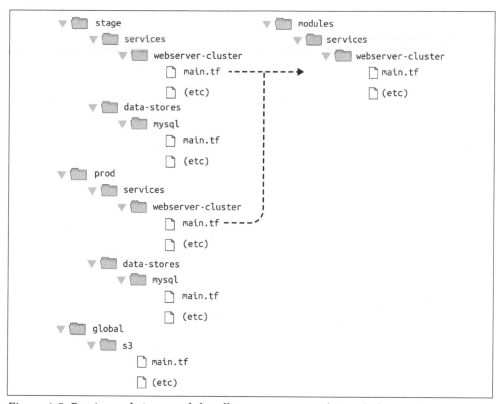

Figure 4-5. Putting code into modules allows you to reuse that code from multiple environments

In this chapter, I'll show you how to create and use Terraform modules by covering the following topics:

- Module basics
- Module inputs
- Module outputs
- Module gotchas
- Module versioning

Example Code

As a reminder, all of the code examples in the book can be found at the following URL: *https://github.com/brikis98/terraform-up-and-running-code*.

Module Basics

A Terraform module is very simple: any set of Terraform configuration files in a folder is a module. All the configurations you've written so far have technically been modules, although not particularly interesting ones, since you deployed them directly (the module in the current working directory is called the *root module*). To see what modules are really capable of, you have to use one module from another module.

As an example, let's turn the code in *stage/services/webserver-cluster*, which includes an Auto Scaling Group (ASG), Elastic Load Balancer (ELB), security groups, and many other resources, into a reusable module.

As a first step, run `terraform destroy` in the *stage/services/webserver-cluster* to clean up any resources you created earlier. Next, create a new top-level folder called *modules* and move all the files from *stage/services/webserver-cluster* to *modules/services/ webserver-cluster*. You should end up with a folder structure that looks something like Figure 4-6.

Open up the *main.tf* file in *modules/services/webserver-cluster* and remove the `pro vider` definition. This should be defined by the user of the module and not in the module itself.

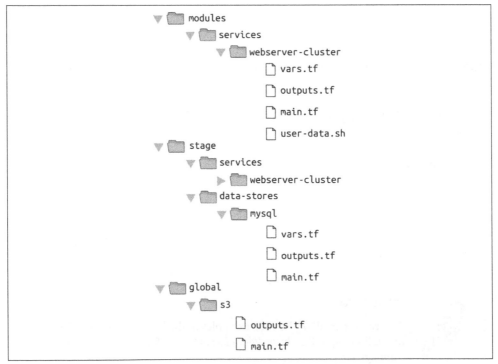

Figure 4-6. The folder structure with a module and a staging environment

You can now make use of this module in the stage environment. The syntax for using a module is:

```
module "NAME" {
  source = "SOURCE"

  [CONFIG ...]
}
```

Within the module definition, the source parameter specifies the folder where the module's code can be found. For example, you can create a new file in *stage/services/webserver-cluster/main.tf* and use the webserver-cluster module in it as follows:

```
provider "aws" {
  region = "us-east-1"
}

module "webserver_cluster" {
  source = "../../../modules/services/webserver-cluster"
}
```

You can then reuse the exact same module in the production environment by creating a new *prod/services/webserver-cluster/main.tf* file with the following contents:

```
provider "aws" {
  region = "us-east-1"
}

module "webserver_cluster" {
  source = "../../../modules/services/webserver-cluster"
}
```

And there you have it: code reuse in multiple environments without any copy/paste! Note that whenever you add a module to your Terraform configurations or modify the source parameter of a module, you need to run the get command before you run plan or apply:

```
> terraform get
Get: /modules/frontend-app

> terraform plan

(...)
```

Before you run the apply command, you should note that there is a problem with the webserver-cluster module: all the names are hard-coded. That is, the name of the security groups, ELB, and other resources are all hard-coded, so if you use this module more than once, you'll get name conflict errors. Even the database details are hard-coded because the *main.tf* file you copied into *modules/services/webserver-cluster* is using a terraform_remote_state data source to figure out the database address and port, and that `terraform_remote_state` is hard-coded to look at the staging environment.

To fix these issues, you need to add configurable inputs to the `webserver-cluster` module so it can behave differently in different environments.

Module Inputs

To make a function configurable in a general-purpose programming language, you can add input parameters to that function:

```
def example_function(param1, param2)
  puts "Hello, #{param1} #{param2}"
end

# Other places in your code
example_function("foo", "bar")
```

In Terraform, modules can have input parameters, too. To define them, you use a mechanism you're already familiar with: input variables. Open up *modules/services/webserver-cluster/vars.tf* and add three new input variables:

```
variable "cluster_name" {
  description = "The name to use for all the cluster resources"
}

variable "db_remote_state_bucket" {
  description = "The name of the S3 bucket for the database's remote state"
}

variable "db_remote_state_key" {
  description = "The path for the database's remote state in S3"
}
```

Next, go through *modules/services/webserver-cluster/main.tf* and use `var.clus ter_name` instead of the hard-coded names (e.g., instead of `"terraform-asg-example"`). For example, here is how you do it for the ELB security group:

```
resource "aws_security_group" "elb" {
  name = "${var.cluster_name}-elb"

  ingress {
    from_port   = 80
    to_port     = 80
    protocol    = "tcp"
    cidr_blocks = ["0.0.0.0/0"]
  }

  egress {
    from_port   = 0
    to_port     = 0
```

```
      protocol    = "-1"
      cidr_blocks = ["0.0.0.0/0"]
    }
  }
```

Notice how the `name` parameter is set to `"${var.cluster_name}"`. You'll need to make a similar change to the other `aws_security_group` resource (e.g., give it the name `"${var.cluster_name}-instance"`), the `aws_elb` resource, and the `tag` section of the `aws_autoscaling_group` resource.

You should also update the `terraform_remote_state` data source to use the `db_remote_state_bucket` and `db_remote_state_key` as its bucket and key parameter, respectively, to ensure you're reading data from the right database:

```
data "terraform_remote_state" "db" {
  backend = "s3"

  config {
    bucket = "${var.db_remote_state_bucket}"
    key    = "${var.db_remote_state_key}"
    region = "us-east-1"
  }
}
```

Now, in the staging environment, you can set these new input variables accordingly:

```
module "webserver_cluster" {
  source = "../../../modules/services/webserver-cluster"

  cluster_name          = "webservers-stage"
  db_remote_state_bucket = "(YOUR_BUCKET_NAME)"
  db_remote_state_key    = "stage/data-stores/mysql/terraform.tfstate"
}
```

You should do the same in the production environment:

```
module "webserver_cluster" {
  source = "../../../modules/services/webserver-cluster"

  cluster_name          = "webservers-prod"
  db_remote_state_bucket = "(YOUR_BUCKET_NAME)"
  db_remote_state_key    = "prod/data-stores/mysql/terraform.tfstate"
}
```

Note: the production database doesn't actually exist yet. As an exercise, I leave it up to you to figure out how to deploy MySQL in both staging and production.

As you can see, you set input variables for a module using the same syntax as setting input parameters for a resource. The input variables are the API of the module, controlling how it will behave in different environments. This example uses different names in different environments, but you may want to make other parameters configurable, too. For example, in staging, you might want to run a small web server cluster to save money, but in production, you might want to run a larger cluster to handle lots of traffic. To do that, you can add three more input variables to *modules/services/webserver-cluster/vars.tf*:

```
variable "instance_type" {
  description = "The type of EC2 Instances to run (e.g. t2.micro)"
}

variable "min_size" {
  description = "The minimum number of EC2 Instances in the ASG"
}

variable "max_size" {
  description = "The maximum number of EC2 Instances in the ASG"
}
```

Next, update the launch configuration in *modules/services/webserver-cluster/main.tf* to set its `instance_type` parameter to the new `var.instance_type` input variable:

```
resource "aws_launch_configuration" "example" {
  image_id        = "ami-40d28157"
  instance_type   = "${var.instance_type}"
  security_groups = ["${aws_security_group.instance.id}"]
  user_data       = "${data.template_file.user_data.rendered}"

  lifecycle {
    create_before_destroy = true
  }
}
```

Similarly, you should update the ASG definition in the same file to set its `min_size` and `max_size` parameters to the new `var.min_size` and `var.max_size` input variables:

```
resource "aws_autoscaling_group" "example" {
  launch_configuration = "${aws_launch_configuration.example.id}"
  availability_zones   = ["${data.aws_availability_zones.all.names}"]
  load_balancers       = ["${aws_elb.example.name}"]
  health_check_type    = "ELB"

  min_size = "${var.min_size}"
  max_size = "${var.max_size}"

  tag {
    key                 = "Name"
    value               = "${var.cluster_name}"
    propagate_at_launch = true
  }
}
```

Now, in the staging environment (*stage/services/webserver-cluster/main.tf*), you can keep the cluster small and inexpensive by setting instance_type to "t2.micro" and min_size and max_size to 2:

```
module "webserver_cluster" {
  source = "../../../modules/services/webserver-cluster"

  cluster_name           = "webservers-stage"
  db_remote_state_bucket = "(YOUR_BUCKET_NAME)"
  db_remote_state_key    = "stage/data-stores/mysql/terraform.tfstate"

  instance_type = "t2.micro"
  min_size      = 2
  max_size      = 2
}
```

On the other hand, in the production environment, you can use a larger instance_type with more CPU and memory, such as m4.large (note: this instance type is *not* part of the AWS free tier, so if you're just using this for learning and don't want to be charged, use "t2.micro" for the instance_type), and you can set max_size to 10 to allow the cluster to shrink or grow depending on the load (don't worry, the cluster will launch with two Instances initially):

```
module "webserver_cluster" {
  source = "../../../modules/services/webserver-cluster"

  cluster_name           = "webservers-prod"
  db_remote_state_bucket = "(YOUR_BUCKET_NAME)"
  db_remote_state_key    = "prod/data-stores/mysql/terraform.tfstate"

  instance_type = "m4.large"
  min_size      = 2
  max_size      = 10
}
```

How do you make the cluster shrink or grow in response to load? One option is to use an *auto scaling schedule*, which can change the size of the cluster at a scheduled time during the day. For example, if traffic to your cluster is much higher during normal business hours, you can use an auto scaling schedule to increase the number of servers at 9 a.m. and decrease it at 5 p.m.

If you define the auto scaling schedule in the webserver-cluster module, it would apply to both staging and production. Since you don't need to do this sort of scaling in your staging environment, for the time being, you can define the auto scaling schedule directly in the production configurations (in Chapter 5, you'll see how to conditionally define resources, which will allow you to move the auto scaling policy into the webserver-cluster module). And to make that work, you're going to have to learn about module outputs.

Module Outputs

To define an auto scaling schedule, add the following two `aws_autoscaling_sched` `ule` resources to *prod/services/webserver-cluster/main.tf*:

```
resource "aws_autoscaling_schedule" "scale_out_during_business_hours" {
  scheduled_action_name = "scale-out-during-business-hours"
  min_size              = 2
  max_size              = 10
  desired_capacity      = 10
  recurrence            = "0 9 * * *"
}

resource "aws_autoscaling_schedule" "scale_in_at_night" {
  scheduled_action_name = "scale-in-at-night"
  min_size              = 2
  max_size              = 10
  desired_capacity      = 2
  recurrence            = "0 17 * * *"
}
```

This code uses one `aws_autoscaling_schedule` resource to increase the number of servers to 10 during the morning hours (the `recurrence` parameter uses cron syntax, so "0 9 * * *" means "9 a.m. every day") and a second `aws_autoscaling_schedule` resource to decrease the number of servers at night ("0 17 * * *" means "5 p.m. every day"). However, both usages of `aws_autoscaling_schedule` are missing a required parameter, `autoscaling_group_name`, which specifies the name of the ASG. The ASG itself is defined within the `webserver-cluster` module, so how do you access its name? In a general-purpose programming language, functions can return values:

```
def example_function(param1, param2)
  return "Hello, #{param1} #{param2}"
end

# Other places in your code
return_value = example_function("foo", "bar")
```

In Terraform, a module can also return values. Again, this is done using a mechanism you already know: output variables. You can add the ASG name as an output variable in */modules/services/webserver-cluster/outputs.tf* as follows:

```
output "asg_name" {
  value = "${aws_autoscaling_group.example.name}"
}
```

You can access module output variables the same way as resource output attributes. The syntax is:

```
"${module.MODULE_NAME.OUTPUT_NAME}"
```

For example:

```
"${module.frontend.asg_name}"
```

In *prod/services/webserver-cluster/main.tf*, you can use this syntax to set the `autoscal
ing_group_name` parameter in each of the `aws_autoscaling_schedule` resources:

```
resource "aws_autoscaling_schedule" "scale_out_during_business_hours" {
  scheduled_action_name = "scale-out-during-business-hours"
  min_size              = 2
  max_size              = 10
  desired_capacity      = 10
  recurrence            = "0 9 * * *"

  autoscaling_group_name = "${module.webserver_cluster.asg_name}"
}

resource "aws_autoscaling_schedule" "scale_in_at_night" {
  scheduled_action_name = "scale-in-at-night"
  min_size              = 2
  max_size              = 10
  desired_capacity      = 2
  recurrence            = "0 17 * * *"

  autoscaling_group_name = "${module.webserver_cluster.asg_name}"
}
```

You may want to expose one other output in the `webserver-cluster` module: the
DNS name of the ELB, so you know what URL to test when the cluster is deployed.
To do that, you again add an output variable in */modules/services/webserver-cluster/
outputs.tf*:

```
output "elb_dns_name" {
  value = "${aws_elb.example.dns_name}"
}
```

You can then "pass through" this output in *stage/services/webserver-cluster/outputs.tf*
and *prod/services/webserver-cluster/outputs.tf* as follows:

```
output "elb_dns_name" {
  value = "${module.webserver_cluster.elb_dns_name}"
}
```

Your web server cluster is almost ready to deploy. The only thing left is to take a few
gotchas into account.

Module Gotchas

When creating modules, watch out for these gotchas:

- File paths
- Inline blocks

File Paths

In Chapter 3, you moved the User Data script for the web server cluster into an external file, *user-data.sh*, and used the `file` interpolation function to read this file from disk. The catch with the `file` function is that the file path you use has to be relative (since you could run Terraform on many different computers)—but what is it relative to?

By default, Terraform interprets the path relative to the current working directory. That works if you're using the `file` function in a Terraform configuration file that's in the same directory as where you're running `terraform apply` (that is, if you're using the `file` function in the root module), but that won't work when you're using `file` in a module that's defined in a separate folder.

To solve this issue, you can use `path.module` to convert to a path that is relative to the module folder. Here is how the `template_file` data source should look in *modules/ services/webserver-cluster/main.tf*:

```
data "template_file" "user_data" {
  template = "${file("${path.module}/user-data.sh")}"

  vars {
    server_port = "${var.server_port}"
    db_address  = "${data.terraform_remote_state.db.address}"
    db_port     = "${data.terraform_remote_state.db.port}"
  }
}
```

Inline Blocks

The configuration for some Terraform resources can be defined either as inline blocks or as separate resources. When creating a module, you should always prefer using a separate resource.

For example, the `aws_security_group` resource allows you to define ingress and egress rules via inline blocks, as you saw in the `webserver-cluster` module (*modules/ services/webserver-cluster/main.tf*):

```
resource "aws_security_group" "elb" {
  name = "${var.cluster_name}-elb"

  ingress {
    from_port   = 80
    to_port     = 80
    protocol    = "tcp"
    cidr_blocks = ["0.0.0.0/0"]
  }

  egress {
    from_port   = 0
    to_port     = 0
    protocol    = "-1"
    cidr_blocks = ["0.0.0.0/0"]
  }
}
```

You should change this module to define the exact same ingress and egress rules by using separate `aws_security_group_rule` resources (make sure to do this for both security groups in the module):

```
resource "aws_security_group" "elb" {
  name = "${var.cluster_name}-elb"
}

resource "aws_security_group_rule" "allow_http_inbound" {
  type              = "ingress"
  security_group_id = "${aws_security_group.elb.id}"

  from_port   = 80
  to_port     = 80
  protocol    = "tcp"
  cidr_blocks = ["0.0.0.0/0"]
}

resource "aws_security_group_rule" "allow_all_outbound" {
  type              = "egress"
  security_group_id = "${aws_security_group.elb.id}"

  from_port   = 0
  to_port     = 0
  protocol    = "-1"
  cidr_blocks = ["0.0.0.0/0"]
}
```

If you try to use a mix of *both* inline blocks and separate resources, you will get errors where routing rules conflict and overwrite each other. Therefore, you must use one or the other. Because of this limitation, when creating a module, you should always try to use a separate resource instead of the inline block. Otherwise, your module will be less flexible and configurable.

For example, if all the ingress and egress rules within the `webserver-cluster` module are defined as separate `aws_security_group_rule` resources, you can make the module flexible enough to allow users to add custom rules from outside of the module. To do that, simply export the ID of the `aws_security_group` as an output variable in *modules/services/webserver-cluster/outputs.tf*:

```
output "elb_security_group_id" {
  value = "${aws_security_group.elb.id}"
}
```

Now, imagine that in the staging environment, you needed to expose an extra port just for testing. This is now easy to do by adding an `aws_security_group_rule` resource to *stage/services/webserver-cluster/main.tf*:

```
resource "aws_security_group_rule" "allow_testing_inbound" {
  type              = "ingress"
  security_group_id = "${module.webserver_cluster.elb_security_group_id}"

  from_port   = 12345
  to_port     = 12345
  protocol    = "tcp"
  cidr_blocks = ["0.0.0.0/0"]
}
```

Had you defined even a single ingress or egress rule as an inline block, this code would not work. Note that this same type of problem affects a number of Terraform resources, such as:

- `aws_security_group` and `aws_security_group_rule`
- `aws_route_table` and `aws_route`
- `aws_network_acl` and `aws_network_acl_rule`
- `aws_elb` and `aws_elb_attachment`

At this point, you are finally ready to deploy your web server cluster in both staging and production. Run the `plan` and `apply` commands as usual and enjoy using two separate copies of your infrastructure.

Network Isolation

The examples in this chapter create two environments that are isolated in your Terraform code, and isolated in terms of having separate load balancers, servers, and databases, but they are not isolated at the network level. To keep all the examples in this book simple, all the resources deploy into the same Virtual Private Cloud (VPC). That means a server in the staging environment can talk to a server in the production environment and vice versa.

In real-world usage, running both environments in one VPC opens you up to two risks. First, a mistake in one environment could affect the other. For example, if you're making changes in staging and accidentally mess up the configuration of the route tables, all the routing in production may be affected too. Second, if an attacker gets access to one environment, they also have access to the other. If you're making rapid changes in staging and accidentally leave a port exposed, any hacker that broke in would not only have access to your staging data, but also your production data.

Therefore, outside of simple examples and experiments, you should run each environment in a separate VPC. In fact, to be extra sure, you may even run each environment in totally separate AWS accounts!

Module Versioning

If both your staging and production environment are pointing to the same module folder, then as soon as you make a change in that folder, it will affect both environments on the very next deployment. This sort of coupling makes it harder to test a change in staging without any chance of affecting production. A better approach is to create *versioned modules* so that you can use one version in staging (e.g., v0.0.2) and a different version in production (e.g., v0.0.1), as shown in Figure 4-7.

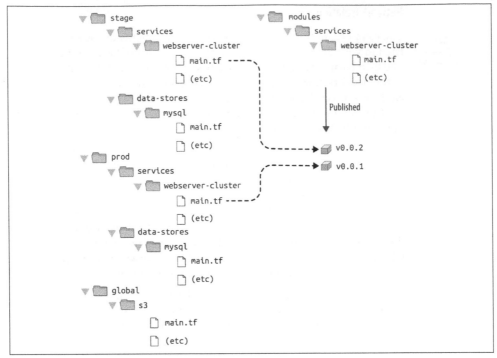

Figure 4-7. Using different versions of a module in different environments

In all the module examples you've seen so far, whenever you used a module, you set the source parameter of the module to a local file path. In addition to file paths, Terraform supports other types of module sources, such as Git URLs, Mercurial URLs, and arbitrary HTTP URLs.[1] The easiest way to create a versioned module is to put the code for the module in a separate Git repository and to set the source parameter to that repository's URL. That means your Terraform code will be spread out across (at least) two repositories:

modules

> This repo defines reusable modules. Think of each module as a "blueprint" that defines a specific part of your infrastructure.

live

> This repo defines the live infrastructure you're running in each environment (stage, prod, mgmt, etc). Think of this as the "houses" you built from the "blueprints" in the *modules* repo.

---

1 For the full details on source URLs, see *https://www.terraform.io/docs/modules/sources.html*.

The updated folder structure for your Terraform code will now look something like Figure 4-8.

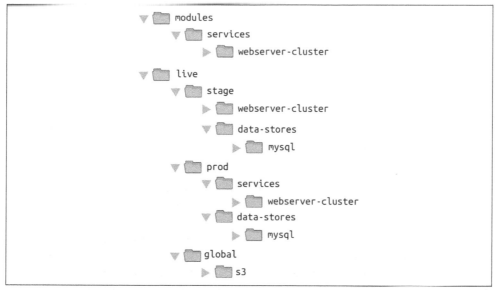

Figure 4-8. File layout with multiple repositories

To set up this folder structure, you'll first need to move the *stage, prod,* and *global* folders into a folder called *live*. Next, configure the *live* and *modules* folders as separate git repositories. Here is an example of how to do that for the *modules* folder:

```
> cd modules
> git init
> git add .
> git commit -m "Initial commit of modules repo"
> git remote add origin "(URL OF REMOTE GIT REPOSITORY)"
> git push origin master
```

You can also add a tag to the *modules* repo to use as a version number. If you're using GitHub, you can use the GitHub UI to create a release, which will create a tag under the hood. If you're not using GitHub, you can use the Git CLI:

```
> git tag -a "v0.0.1" -m "First release of webserver-cluster module"
> git push --follow-tags
```

Now you can use this versioned module in both staging and production by specifying a Git URL in the source parameter. Here is what that would look like in *live/stage/ services/webserver-cluster/main.tf* if your modules repo was in the GitHub repo *github.com/foo/modules* (note that the double-slash in the Git URL is required):

```
module "webserver_cluster" {
  source = "git::git@github.com:foo/modules.git//webserver-cluster?ref=v0.0.1"

  cluster_name            = "webservers-stage"
  db_remote_state_bucket = "(YOUR_BUCKET_NAME)"
  db_remote_state_key     = "stage/data-stores/mysql/terraform.tfstate"

  instance_type = "t2.micro"
  min_size      = 2
  max_size      = 2
}
```

If you want to try out versioned modules without messing with Git repos, you can use a module from the code examples GitHub repo for this book (I had to break up the URL to make it fit in the book, but it should all be on one line):

```
source = "git@github.com:brikis98/terraform-up-and-running-code.git//
    code/terraform/04-terraform-module/module-example/modules/
    services/webserver-cluster?ref=v0.0.2"
```

The `ref` parameter allows you to specify a specific Git commit via its sha1 hash, a branch name, or, as in this example, a specific Git tag. I generally recommend using Git tags as version numbers for modules. Branch names are not stable, as you always get the latest commit on a branch, which may change every time you run the `get` command, and the sha1 hashes are not very human friendly. Git tags are as stable as a commit (in fact, a tag is just a pointer to a commit) but they allow you to use any name you want.

A particularly useful naming scheme for tags is *semantic versioning* (*http://semver.org*). This is a versioning scheme of the format `MAJOR.MINOR.PATCH` (e.g., `1.0.4`) with specific rules on when you should increment each part of the version number. In particular, you should increment the…

- MAJOR version when you make incompatible API changes,
- MINOR version when you add functionality in a backward-compatible manner, and
- PATCH version when you make backward-compatible bug fixes.

Semantic versioning gives you a way to communicate to users of your module what kind of changes you've made and the implications of upgrading.

Since you've updated your Terraform code to use a versioned module URL, you need to run `terraform get -update`:

```
> terraform get -update
Get: git::ssh://git@github.com/foo/modules.git?ref=v0.0.1

> terraform plan
(...)
```

This time, you can see that Terraform downloads the module code from Git rather than your local filesystem. Once the module code has been downloaded, you can run the plan and apply commands as usual.

Private Git Repos

If your Terraform module is in a private Git repository, you will need to ensure the computer you're using has SSH keys configured correctly that allow Terraform to access that repository. In other words, before using the URL *ssh://git@github.com/foo/modules.git* in the source parameter of your module, make sure you can git clone that URL in your terminal:

```
> git clone ssh://git@github.com/foo/modules.git
```

If that command fails, you need to set up your SSH keys first. Git-Hub has excellent documentation on how to do that (*https://help.github.com/articles/generating-an-ssh-key*).

Now, imagine you made some changes to the webserver-cluster module and you wanted to test them out in staging. First, you'd commit those changes to the *modules* repo:

```
> cd modules
> git add .
> git commit -m "Made some changes to webserver-cluster"
> git push origin master
```

Next, you would create a new tag in the *modules* repo:

```
> git tag -a "v0.0.2" -m "Second release of webserver-cluster"
> git push --follow-tags
```

And now you can update *just* the source URL used in the staging environment (*live/stage/services/webserver-cluster/main.tf*) to use this new version:

```
module "webserver_cluster" {
  source = "git::git@github.com:foo/modules.git//webserver-cluster?ref=v0.0.2"

  cluster_name          = "webservers-stage"
  db_remote_state_bucket = "(YOUR_BUCKET_NAME)"
  db_remote_state_key   = "stage/data-stores/mysql/terraform.tfstate"

  instance_type = "t2.micro"
  min_size      = 2
  max_size      = 2
}
```

In production (*live/prod/services/webserver-cluster/main.tf*), you can happily continue to run v0.0.1 unchanged:

```
module "webserver_cluster" {
  source = "git::git@github.com:foo/modules.git//webserver-cluster?ref=v0.0.1"

  cluster_name           = "webservers-prod"
  db_remote_state_bucket = "(YOUR_BUCKET_NAME)"
  db_remote_state_key    = "prod/data-stores/mysql/terraform.tfstate"

  instance_type = "m4.large"
  min_size      = 2
  max_size      = 10
}
```

Once v0.0.2 has been thoroughly tested and proven in staging, you can then update production, too. But if there turns out to be a bug in v0.0.2, no big deal, as it has no effect on live users. Fix the bug, release a new version, and repeat the whole process again until you have something stable enough for production.

Developing Modules

Versioned modules are great when you're deploying to a shared environment (e.g., staging or production), but when you're just testing on your own computer, you'll want to use local file paths. This allows you to iterate faster, as you'll be able to make a change in the module folders and rerun the plan or apply command in the live folders immediately, rather than having to commit your code and publish a new version each time.

Since the goal of this book is to help you learn and experiment with Terraform as quickly as possible, the rest of the code examples will use local file paths for modules.

Conclusion

By defining infrastructure as code in modules, you can apply a variety of software engineering best practices to your infrastructure. You can validate each change to a module through code reviews and automated tests; you can create semantically versioned releases of each module; and you can safely try out different versions of a module in different environments and roll back to previous versions if you hit a problem.

All of this can dramatically increase your ability to build infrastructure quickly and reliably, as developers will be able to reuse entire pieces of proven, tested, documented infrastructure. For example, you could create a canonical module that defines how to deploy a single microservice—including how to run a cluster, how to scale the cluster in response to load, and how to distribute traffic requests across the cluster—and each team could use this module to manage their own microservices with just a few lines of code.

To make such a module work for multiple teams, the Terraform code in that module must be flexible and configurable. For example, one team may want to use your module to deploy a single instance of their microservice with no load balancer while another may want a dozen instances of their microservice with a load balancer to distribute traffic between those instances. How do you do conditional statements in Terraform? Is there a way to do a for-loop? Is there a way to use Terraform to roll out changes to this microservice without downtime? These advanced aspects of Terraform syntax are the topic of Chapter 5.

## CHAPTER 5

Terraform Tips and Tricks: Loops, If-Statements, Deployment, and Gotchas

Terraform is a declarative language. As discussed in Chapter 1, infrastructure as code in a declarative language tends to provide a more accurate view of what's actually deployed than a procedural language, so it's easier to reason about and makes it easier to keep the codebase small. However, certain types of tasks are more difficult in a declarative language.

For example, since declarative languages typically don't have for-loops, how do you repeat a piece of logic—such as creating multiple similar resources—without copy and paste? And if the declarative language doesn't support if-statements, how can you conditionally configure resources, such as creating a Terraform module that can create certain resources for some users of that module but not for others? Finally, how do you express an inherently procedural idea, such as a zero-downtime deployment, in a declarative language?

Fortunately, Terraform provides a few primitives—namely, a meta-parameter called count, a lifecycle block called create_before_destroy, a ternary operator, plus a large number of interpolation functions—that allow you to do certain types of loops, if-statements, and zero-downtime deployments. You probably won't need to use these too often, but when you do, it's good to be aware of what's possible and what the gotchas are. Here are the topics I'll cover in this chapter:

- Loops
- If-statements
- If-else-statements

- Zero-downtime deployment
- Terraform gotchas

Example Code

As a reminder, all of the code examples in the book can be found at the following URL: *https://github.com/brikis98/terraform-up-and-running-code*.

Loops

In Chapter 2, you created an IAM user by clicking around the AWS console. Now that you have this user, you can create and manage all future IAM users with Terraform. Consider the following Terraform code, which should live in *live/global/iam/main.tf*:

```
provider "aws" {
  region = "us-east-1"
}

resource "aws_iam_user" "example" {
  name = "neo"
}
```

This code uses the `aws_iam_user` resource to create a single new IAM user. What if you wanted to create three IAM users? In a general-purpose programming language, you'd probably use a for-loop:

```
# This is just pseudo code. It won't actually work in Terraform.
for i = 0; i < 3; i++ {
  resource "aws_iam_user" "example" {
    name = "neo"
  }
}
```

Terraform does not have for-loops or other traditional procedural logic built into the language, so this syntax will not work. However, almost every Terraform resource has a meta-parameter you can use called count. This parameter defines how many copies of the resource to create. Therefore, you can create three IAM users as follows:

```
resource "aws_iam_user" "example" {
  count = 3
  name  = "neo"
}
```

One problem with this code is that all three IAM users would have the same name, which would cause an error, since usernames must be unique. If you had access to a standard for-loop, you might use the index in the for loop, i, to give each user a unique name:

```
# This is just pseudo code. It won't actually work in Terraform.
for i = 0; i < 3; i++ {
  resource "aws_iam_user" "example" {
    name = "neo.${i}"
  }
}
```

To accomplish the same thing in Terraform, you can use `count.index` to get the index of each "iteration" in the "loop":

```
resource "aws_iam_user" "example" {
  count = 3
  name  = "neo.${count.index}"
}
```

If you run the `plan` command on the preceding code, you will see that Terraform wants to create three IAM users, each with a different name ("neo.0", "neo.1", "neo.2"):

```
+ aws_iam_user.example.0
    arn:            "<computed>"
    force_destroy:  "false"
    name:           "neo.0"
    path:           "/"
    unique_id:      "<computed>"

+ aws_iam_user.example.1
    arn:            "<computed>"
    force_destroy:  "false"
    name:           "neo.1"
    path:           "/"
    unique_id:      "<computed>"

+ aws_iam_user.example.2
    arn:            "<computed>"
    force_destroy:  "false"
    name:           "neo.2"
    path:           "/"
    unique_id:      "<computed>"


Plan: 3 to add, 0 to change, 0 to destroy.
```

Of course, a username like "neo.0" isn't particularly usable. If you combine `count.index` with some interpolation functions built into Terraform, you can customize each "iteration" of the "loop" even more.

For example, you could define all of the IAM usernames you want in an input variable in *live/global/iam/vars.tf*:

```
variable "user_names" {
  description = "Create IAM users with these names"
  type        = "list"
  default     = ["neo", "trinity", "morpheus"]
}
```

If you were using a general-purpose programming language with loops and arrays, you would configure each IAM user to use a different name by looking up index i in the array var.user_names:

```
# This is just pseudo code. It won't actually work in Terraform.
for i = 0; i < 3; i++ {
  resource "aws_iam_user" "example" {
    name = "${vars.user_names[i]}"
  }
}
```

In Terraform, you can accomplish the same thing by using count and two interpolation functions, element and length:

```
"${element(LIST, INDEX)}"
"${length(LIST)}"
```

The element function returns the item located at INDEX in the given LIST.[1] The length function returns the number of items in LIST (it also works with strings and maps). Putting these together, you get:

```
resource "aws_iam_user" "example" {
  count = "${length(var.user_names)}"
  name  = "${element(var.user_names, count.index)}"
}
```

Now when you run the plan command, you'll see that Terraform wants to create three IAM users, each with a unique name:

```
+ aws_iam_user.example.0
    arn:           "<computed>"
    force_destroy: "false"
    name:          "neo"
    path:          "/"
    unique_id:     "<computed>"

+ aws_iam_user.example.1
    arn:           "<computed>"
    force_destroy: "false"
    name:          "trinity"
    path:          "/"
    unique_id:     "<computed>"
```

---

1 If the index is greater than the number of elements in list, the element function will automatically "wrap" around using a standard mod function.

```
+ aws_iam_user.example.2
    arn:              "<computed>"
    force_destroy:    "false"
    name:             "morpheus"
    path:             "/"
    unique_id:        "<computed>"


Plan: 3 to add, 0 to change, 0 to destroy.
```

Note that once you've used count on a resource, it becomes a list of resources, rather than just one resource. Since aws_iam_user.example is now a list of IAM users, instead of using the standard syntax to read an attribute from that resource (TYPE.NAME.ATTRIBUTE), you have to specify which IAM user you're interested in by specifying its index in the list:

```
"${TYPE.NAME.INDEX.ATTRIBUTE}"
```

For example, if you wanted to provide the Amazon Resource Name (ARN) of one of the IAM users as an output variable, you would need to do the following:

```
output "neo_arn" {
  value = "${aws_iam_user.example.0.arn}"
}
```

If you want the ARNs of *all* the IAM users, you need to use the *splat* character, "*", instead of the index:

```
"${aws_iam_user.example.*.arn}"
```

When you use the splat character, you get back a list, so you need to wrap the output variable with brackets:

```
output "all_arns" {
  value = ["${aws_iam_user.example.*.arn}"]
}
```

When you run the apply command, the all_arns output will contain the list of ARNs:

```
> terraform apply

(...)

Apply complete! Resources: 3 added, 0 changed, 0 destroyed.

Outputs:

all_arns = [
    arn:aws:iam::123456789012:user/neo,
    arn:aws:iam::123456789012:user/trinity,
```

```
      arn:aws:iam::123456789012:user/morpheus
]
```

Note that since the splat syntax returns a list, you can combine it with other interpolation functions, such as `element`. For example, let's say you wanted to give each of these IAM users read-only access to EC2. You may remember from Chapter 2 that by default, new IAM users have no permissions whatsoever, and that to grant permissions, you can attach IAM policies to those IAM users. An IAM policy is a JSON document:

```
{
  "Statement": [
    {
      "Effect": "Allow",
      "Action": ["ec2:Describe*"],
      "Resource": ["*"]
    }
  ]
}
```

An IAM policy consists of one or more *statements*, each of which specifies an *effect* (either "Allow" or "Deny"), on one or more *actions* (e.g., `"ec2:Describe*"` allows all API calls to EC2 that start with the name `"Describe"`), on one or more *resources* (e.g., `"*"` means "all resources"). Although you can define IAM policies in JSON, Terraform also provides a handy data source called the `aws_iam_policy_document` that gives you a more concise way to define the same IAM policy:

```
data "aws_iam_policy_document" "ec2_read_only" {
  statement {
    effect    = "Allow"
    actions   = ["ec2:Describe*"]
    resources = ["*"]
  }
}
```

To create a new managed IAM policy from this document, you need to use the `aws_iam_policy` resource and set its `policy` parameter to the JSON output of the `aws_iam_policy_document` you just created:

```
resource "aws_iam_policy" "ec2_read_only" {
  name   = "ec2-read-only"
  policy = "${data.aws_iam_policy_document.ec2_read_only.json}"
}
```

Finally, to attach the IAM policy to your new IAM users, you use the `aws_iam_user_policy_attachment` resource:

```
resource "aws_iam_user_policy_attachment" "ec2_access" {
  count = "${length(var.user_names)}"
  user  = "${element(aws_iam_user.example.*.name, count.index)}"
```

```
  policy_arn = "${aws_iam_policy.ec2_read_only.arn}"
}
```

This code uses the count parameter to "loop" over each of your IAM users and the element interpolation function to select each user's ARN from the list returned by aws_iam_user.example.*.arn.

If-Statements

Using count lets you do a basic loop. If you're clever, you can use the same mechanism to do a basic if-statement as well. Let's start by looking at simple if-statements in the next section and then move on to more complicated ones in the section after that.

Simple If-Statements

In Chapter 4, you created a Terraform module that could be used as "blueprint" for deploying web server clusters. The module created an Auto Scaling Group (ASG), Elastic Load Balancer (ELB), security groups, and a number of other resources. One thing the module did *not* create was the auto scaling schedule. Since you only want to scale the cluster out in production, you defined the aws_autoscaling_schedule resources directly in the production configurations under *live/prod/services/ webserver-cluster/main.tf*. Is there a way you could define the aws_autoscal ing_schedule resources in the webserver-cluster module and conditionally create them for some users of the module and not create them for others?

Let's give it a shot. The first step is to add a boolean input variable in *modules/services/webserver-cluster/vars.tf* that can be used to specify whether the module should enable auto scaling:

```
variable "enable_autoscaling" {
  description = "If set to true, enable auto scaling"
}
```

Now, if you had a general-purpose programming language, you could use this input variable in an if-statement:

```
# This is just pseudo code. It won't actually work in Terraform.
if ${var.enable_autoscaling} {
  resource "aws_autoscaling_schedule" "scale_out_during_business_hours" {
    scheduled_action_name  = "scale-out-during-business-hours"
    min_size               = 2
    max_size               = 10
    desired_capacity       = 10
    recurrence             = "0 9 * * *"
    autoscaling_group_name = "${aws_autoscaling_group.example.name}"
  }

  resource "aws_autoscaling_schedule" "scale_in_at_night" {
```

```
    scheduled_action_name  = "scale-in-at-night"
    min_size               = 2
    max_size               = 10
    desired_capacity       = 2
    recurrence             = "0 17 * * *"
    autoscaling_group_name = "${aws_autoscaling_group.example.name}"
  }
}
```

Terraform doesn't support if-statements, so this code won't work. However, you can accomplish the same thing by using the `count` parameter and taking advantage of two properties:

1. In Terraform, if you set a variable to a boolean `true` (that is, the word `true` without any quotes around it), it will be coerced into a 1, and if you set it to a boolean `false`, it will be coerced into a 0.

2. If you set `count` to 1 on a resource, you get one copy of that resource; if you set `count` to 0, that resource is not created at all.

Putting these two ideas together, you can update the `webserver-cluster` module as follows:

```
resource "aws_autoscaling_schedule" "scale_out_during_business_hours" {
  count = "${var.enable_autoscaling}"

  scheduled_action_name  = "scale-out-during-business-hours"
  min_size               = 2
  max_size               = 10
  desired_capacity       = 10
  recurrence             = "0 9 * * *"
  autoscaling_group_name = "${aws_autoscaling_group.example.name}"
}

resource "aws_autoscaling_schedule" "scale_in_at_night" {
  count = "${var.enable_autoscaling}"

  scheduled_action_name  = "scale-in-at-night"
  min_size               = 2
  max_size               = 10
  desired_capacity       = 2
  recurrence             = "0 17 * * *"
  autoscaling_group_name = "${aws_autoscaling_group.example.name}"
}
```

If `var.enable_autoscaling` is `true`, the `count` parameter for each of the `aws_autoscaling_schedule` resources will be set to 1, so one of each will be created. If `var.enable_autoscaling` is `false`, the `count` parameter for each of the `aws_autoscaling_schedule` resources will be set to 0, so neither one will be created. This is exactly the conditional logic you want!

You can now update the usage of this module in staging (in *live/stage/services/webserver-cluster/main.tf*) to disable auto scaling by setting enable_autoscaling to false:

```
module "webserver_cluster" {
  source = "../../../../modules/services/webserver-cluster"

  cluster_name          = "webservers-stage"
  db_remote_state_bucket = "(YOUR_BUCKET_NAME)"
  db_remote_state_key   = "stage/data-stores/mysql/terraform.tfstate"

  instance_type         = "t2.micro"
  min_size              = 2
  max_size              = 2
  enable_autoscaling    = false
}
```

Similarly, you can update the usage of this module in production (in *live/prod/services/webserver-cluster/main.tf*) to enable auto scaling by setting enable_autoscaling to true (make sure to also remove the custom aws_autoscaling_schedule resources that were in the production environment from Chapter 4):

```
module "webserver_cluster" {
  source = "../../../../modules/services/webserver-cluster"

  cluster_name          = "webservers-prod"
  db_remote_state_bucket = "(YOUR_BUCKET_NAME)"
  db_remote_state_key   = "prod/data-stores/mysql/terraform.tfstate"

  instance_type         = "m4.large"
  min_size              = 2
  max_size              = 10
  enable_autoscaling    = true
}
```

More Complicated If-Statements

This approach works well if the user passes an explicit boolean value to your module, but what do you do if the boolean is the result of a more complicated comparison, such as string equality? To handle more complicated cases, you can again use the count parameter, but this time, rather than setting it to a boolean variable, you set it to the value returned by a *conditional*. Conditionals in Terraform use the same *ternary syntax* available in many programming languages:

```
"${CONDITION ? TRUEVAL : FALSEVAL}"
```

For example, a more verbose way to do the simple if-statement from the previous section is as follows:

```
count = "${var.enable_autoscaling ? 1 : 0}"
```

Let's go through a more complicated example. Imagine that as part of the `webserver-cluster` module, you wanted to create a set of CloudWatch alarms. A *CloudWatch alarm* can be configured to notify you via a variety of mechanisms (e.g., email, text message) if a specific metric exceeds a predefined threshold. For example, here is how you could use the `aws_cloudwatch_metric_alarm` resource in *modules/services/webserver-cluster/main.tf* to create an alarm that goes off if the average CPU utilization in the cluster is over 90% during a 5-minute period:

```
resource "aws_cloudwatch_metric_alarm" "high_cpu_utilization" {
  alarm_name  = "${var.cluster_name}-high-cpu-utilization"
  namespace   = "AWS/EC2"
  metric_name = "CPUUtilization"

  dimensions = {
    AutoScalingGroupName = "${aws_autoscaling_group.example.name}"
  }

  comparison_operator = "GreaterThanThreshold"
  evaluation_periods  = 1
  period              = 300
  statistic           = "Average"
  threshold           = 90
  unit                = "Percent"
}
```

This works fine for a CPU Utilization alarm, but what if you wanted to add another alarm that goes off when CPU credits are low?[2] Here is a CloudWatch alarm that goes off if your web server cluster is almost out of CPU credits:

```
resource "aws_cloudwatch_metric_alarm" "low_cpu_credit_balance" {
  alarm_name  = "${var.cluster_name}-low-cpu-credit-balance"
  namespace   = "AWS/EC2"
  metric_name = "CPUCreditBalance"

  dimensions = {
    AutoScalingGroupName = "${aws_autoscaling_group.example.name}"
  }

  comparison_operator = "LessThanThreshold"
  evaluation_periods  = 1
  period              = 300
  statistic           = "Minimum"
  threshold           = 10
  unit                = "Count"
}
```

---

2 You can learn about CPU credits here: *http://amzn.to/2lTuvs5*.

The catch is that CPU credits only apply to tXXX Instances (e.g., t2.micro, t2.medium, etc). Larger instance types (e.g., m4.large) don't use CPU credits and don't report a CPUCreditBalance metric, so if you create such an alarm for those instances, the alarm will always be stuck in the "INSUFFICIENT_DATA" state. Is there a way to create an alarm only if var.instance_type starts with the letter "t"?

You could add a new boolean input variable called var.is_t2_instance, but that would be redundant with var.instance_type, and you'd most likely forget to update one when updating the other. A better alternative is to use a conditional:

```
resource "aws_cloudwatch_metric_alarm" "low_cpu_credit_balance" {
  count = "${format("%.1s", var.instance_type) == "t" ? 1 : 0}"

  alarm_name  = "${var.cluster_name}-low-cpu-credit-balance"
  namespace   = "AWS/EC2"
  metric_name = "CPUCreditBalance"

  dimensions = {
    AutoScalingGroupName = "${aws_autoscaling_group.example.name}"
  }

  comparison_operator = "LessThanThreshold"
  evaluation_periods  = 1
  period              = 300
  statistic           = "Minimum"
  threshold           = 10
  unit                = "Count"
}
```

The alarm code is the same as before, except for the relatively complicated count parameter:

```
count = "${format("%.1s", var.instance_type) == "t" ? 1 : 0}"
```

This code uses the format function to extract just the first character from var.instance_type. If that character is a "t" (e.g., t2.micro), it sets the count to 1; otherwise, it sets the count to 0. This way, the alarm is only created for instance types that actually have a CPUCreditBalance metric.

If-Else-Statements

Now that you know how to do an if-statement, what about an if-else-statement? Let's again start by looking at simple if-else-statements in the next section and move on to more complicated ones in the section after that.

Simple If-Else-Statements

Earlier in this chapter, you created several IAM users with read-only access to EC2. Imagine that you wanted to give one of these users, neo, access to CloudWatch as well, but to allow the person applying the Terraform configurations to decide if neo got only read access or both read and write access. This is a slightly contrived example, but it makes it easy to demonstrate a simple type of if-else-statement, where all that matters is that one of the if or else branches gets executed, and the rest of the Terraform code doesn't need to know which one.

Here is an IAM policy that allows read-only access to CloudWatch:

```
resource "aws_iam_policy" "cloudwatch_read_only" {
  name   = "cloudwatch-read-only"
  policy = "${data.aws_iam_policy_document.cloudwatch_read_only.json}"
}

data "aws_iam_policy_document" "cloudwatch_read_only" {
  statement {
    effect    = "Allow"
    actions   = ["cloudwatch:Describe*", "cloudwatch:Get*", "cloudwatch:List*"]
    resources = ["*"]
  }
}
```

And here is an IAM policy that allows full (read and write) access to CloudWatch:

```
resource "aws_iam_policy" "cloudwatch_full_access" {
  name   = "cloudwatch-full-access"
  policy = "${data.aws_iam_policy_document.cloudwatch_full_access.json}"
}

data "aws_iam_policy_document" "cloudwatch_full_access" {
  statement {
    effect    = "Allow"
    actions   = ["cloudwatch:*"]
    resources = ["*"]
  }
}
```

The goal is to attach one of these IAM policies to neo, based on the value of a new input variable called give_neo_cloudwatch_full_access:

```
variable "give_neo_cloudwatch_full_access" {
  description = "If true, neo gets full access to CloudWatch"
}
```

If you were using a general-purpose programming language, you might write an if-else-statement that looks like this:

```
# This is just pseudo code. It won't actually work in Terraform.
if ${var.give_neo_cloudwatch_full_access} {
  resource "aws_iam_user_policy_attachment" "neo_cloudwatch_full_access" {
    user       = "${aws_iam_user.example.0.name}"
    policy_arn = "${aws_iam_policy.cloudwatch_full_access.arn}"
  }
} else {
  resource "aws_iam_user_policy_attachment" "neo_cloudwatch_read_only" {
    user       = "${aws_iam_user.example.0.name}"
    policy_arn = "${aws_iam_policy.cloudwatch_read_only.arn}"
  }
}
```

To do this in Terraform, you can again use the count parameter and a boolean, but this time, you also need to take advantage of the fact that Terraform allows simple math in interpolations:

```
resource "aws_iam_user_policy_attachment" "neo_cloudwatch_full_access" {
  count = "${var.give_neo_cloudwatch_full_access}"

  user       = "${aws_iam_user.example.0.name}"
  policy_arn = "${aws_iam_policy.cloudwatch_full_access.arn}"
}

resource "aws_iam_user_policy_attachment" "neo_cloudwatch_read_only" {
  count = "${1 - var.give_neo_cloudwatch_full_access}"

  user       = "${aws_iam_user.example.0.name}"
  policy_arn = "${aws_iam_policy.cloudwatch_read_only.arn}"
}
```

This code contains two aws_iam_user_policy_attachment resources. The first one, which attaches the CloudWatch full access permissions, sets its count parameter to var.give_neo_cloudwatch_full_access, so this resource only gets created if var.give_neo_cloudwatch_full_access is true (this is the if-clause). The second one, which attaches the CloudWatch read-only permissions, sets its count parameter to 1 - var.give_neo_cloudwatch_full_access, so it will have the inverse behavior, and only be created if var.give_neo_cloudwatch_full_access is false (this is the else-clause).

More Complicated If-Else-Statements

This approach works well if your Terraform code doesn't need to know which of the if or else clauses actually got executed. But what if you need to access some output attribute on the resource that comes out of the if or else clause? For example, what if you wanted to offer two different User Data scripts in the webserver-cluster module and allow users to pick which one gets executed? Currently, the webserver-cluster module pulls in the *user-data.sh* script via a template_file data source:

```
data "template_file" "user_data" {
  template = "${file("${path.module}/user-data.sh")}"

  vars {
    server_port = "${var.server_port}"
    db_address  = "${data.terraform_remote_state.db.address}"
    db_port     = "${data.terraform_remote_state.db.port}"
  }
}
```

The current *user-data.sh* script looks like this:

```
#!/bin/bash

cat > index.html <<EOF
<h1>Hello, World</h1>
<p>DB address: ${db_address}</p>
<p>DB port: ${db_port}</p>
EOF

nohup busybox httpd -f -p "${server_port}" &
```

Now, imagine that you wanted to allow some of your web server clusters to use this alternative, shorter script, called *user-data-new.sh*:

```
#!/bin/bash

echo "Hello, World, v2" > index.html
nohup busybox httpd -f -p "${server_port}" &
```

To use this script, you need a new `template_file` data source:

```
data "template_file" "user_data_new" {
  template = "${file("${path.module}/user-data-new.sh")}"

  vars {
    server_port = "${var.server_port}"
  }
}
```

The question is, how can you allow the user of the `webserver-cluster` module to pick from one of these User Data scripts? As a first step, you could add a new boolean input variable in *modules/services/webserver-cluster/vars.tf*:

```
variable "enable_new_user_data" {
  description = "If set to true, use the new User Data script"
}
```

If you were using a general-purpose programming language, you could add an if-else-statement to the launch configuration to pick between the two User Data `template_file` options as follows:

```
# This is just pseudo code. It won't actually work in Terraform.
resource "aws_launch_configuration" "example" {
  image_id        = "ami-40d28157"
  instance_type   = "${var.instance_type}"
  security_groups = ["${aws_security_group.instance.id}"]

  if ${var.enable_new_user_data} {
    user_data = "${data.template_file.user_data_new.rendered}"
  } else {
    user_data = "${data.template_file.user_data.rendered}"
  }

  lifecycle {
    create_before_destroy = true
  }
}
```

To make this work with real Terraform code, you first need to use the if-else-statement trick from before to ensure that only one of the `template_file` data sources is actually created:

```
data "template_file" "user_data" {
  count = "${1 - var.enable_new_user_data}"

  template = "${file("${path.module}/user-data.sh")}"

  vars {
    server_port = "${var.server_port}"
    db_address  = "${data.terraform_remote_state.db.address}"
    db_port     = "${data.terraform_remote_state.db.port}"
  }
}

data "template_file" "user_data_new" {
  count = "${var.enable_new_user_data}"

  template = "${file("${path.module}/user-data-new.sh")}"

  vars {
    server_port = "${var.server_port}"
  }
}
```

If `var.enable_new_user_data` is `true`, then `data.template_file.user_data_new` will be created and `data.template_file.user_data` will not; if it's `false`, it'll be the other way around. All you have to do now is to set the `user_data` parameter of the `aws_launch_configuration` resource to the `template_file` that actually exists. To do this, you can take advantage of the `concat` interpolation function:

```
"${concat(LIST1, LIST2, ...)}"
```

The concat function combines two or more lists into a single list. Here is how you can combine it with the element function to select the proper template_file:

```
resource "aws_launch_configuration" "example" {
  image_id        = "ami-40d28157"
  instance_type   = "${var.instance_type}"
  security_groups = ["${aws_security_group.instance.id}"]

  user_data = "${element(
    concat(data.template_file.user_data.*.rendered,
           data.template_file.user_data_new.*.rendered),
    0)}"

  lifecycle {
    create_before_destroy = true
  }
}
```

Let's break the large value for the user_data parameter down. First, take a look at the inner part:

```
concat(data.template_file.user_data.*.rendered,
       data.template_file.user_data_new.*.rendered)
```

Note that the two template_file resources are both lists, as they both use the count parameter. One of these lists will be of length 1 and the other of length 0, depending on the value of var.enable_new_user_data. The preceding code uses the concat function to combine these two lists into a single list, which will be of length 1. Now consider the outer part:

```
user_data =  "${element(<INNER>, 0)}"
```

This code simply takes the list returned by the inner part, which will be of length 1, and uses the element function to extract that one value.

You can now try out the new User Data script in the staging environment by setting the enable_new_user_data parameter to true in *live/stage/services/webserver-cluster/main.tf*:

```
module "webserver_cluster" {
  source = "../../../../modules/services/webserver-cluster"

  cluster_name          = "webservers-stage"
  db_remote_state_bucket = "(YOUR_BUCKET_NAME)"
  db_remote_state_key   = "stage/data-stores/mysql/terraform.tfstate"

  instance_type         = "t2.micro"
  min_size              = 2
  max_size              = 2
  enable_autoscaling    = false
  enable_new_user_data  = true
}
```

In the production environment, you can stick with the old version of the script by setting `enable_new_user_data` to `false` in *live/prod/services/webserver-cluster/ main.tf*:

```
module "webserver_cluster" {
  source = "../../../../modules/services/webserver-cluster"

  cluster_name           = "webservers-prod"
  db_remote_state_bucket = "(YOUR_BUCKET_NAME)"
  db_remote_state_key    = "prod/data-stores/mysql/terraform.tfstate"

  instance_type         = "m4.large"
  min_size              = 2
  max_size              = 10
  enable_autoscaling    = true
  enable_new_user_data  = false
}
```

Using count and interpolation functions to simulate if-else-statements is a bit of a hack, but it's one that works fairly well, and as you can see from the code, it allows you to conceal lots of complexity from your users so that they get to work with a clean and simple API.

Zero-Downtime Deployment

Now that your module has a clean and simple API for deploying a web server cluster, an important question to ask is, how do you update that cluster? That is, when you have made changes to your code, how do you deploy a new AMI across the cluster? And how do you do it without causing downtime for your users?

The first step is to expose the AMI as an input variable in *modules/services/webserver-cluster/vars.tf*. In real-world examples, this is all you would need, as the actual web server code would be defined in the AMI. However, in the simplified examples in this book, all of the web server code is actually in the User Data script, and the AMI is just a vanilla Ubuntu image. Switching to a different version of Ubuntu won't make for much of a demonstration, so in addition to the new AMI input variable, you can also add an input variable to control the text the User Data script returns from its one-liner HTTP server:

```
variable "ami" {
  description = "The AMI to run in the cluster"
  default     = "ami-40d28157"
}

variable "server_text" {
  description = "The text the web server should return"
  default     = "Hello, World"
}
```

Earlier in the chapter, to practice with if-else-statements, you created two User Data scripts. Let's consolidate that back down to one to keep things simple. First, in *modules/services/webserver-cluster/vars.tf*, remove the `enable_new_user_data` input variable. Second, in *modules/services/webserver-cluster/main.tf*, remove the `tem plate_file` resource called `user_data_new`. Third, in the same file, update the other `template_file` resource, called `user_data`, to no longer use the `enable_new_user_data` input variable, and to add the new `server_text` input variable to its `vars` block:

```
data "template_file" "user_data" {
  template = "${file("${path.module}/user-data.sh")}"

  vars {
    server_port = "${var.server_port}"
    db_address  = "${data.terraform_remote_state.db.address}"
    db_port     = "${data.terraform_remote_state.db.port}"
    server_text = "${var.server_text}"
  }
}
```

Now you need to update the *modules/services/webserver-cluster/user-data.sh* Bash script to use this `server_text` variable in the <h1> tag it returns:

```
#!/bin/bash

cat > index.html <<EOF
<h1>${server_text}</h1>
<p>DB address: ${db_address}</p>
<p>DB port: ${db_port}</p>
EOF

nohup busybox httpd -f -p "${server_port}" &
```

Finally, find the launch configuration in *modules/services/webserver-cluster/main.tf*, set its `user_data` parameter to the remaining `template_file` (the one called `user_data`), and set its `ami` parameter to the new `ami` input variable:

```
resource "aws_launch_configuration" "example" {
  image_id        = "${var.ami}"
  instance_type   = "${var.instance_type}"
  security_groups = ["${aws_security_group.instance.id}"]

  user_data = "${data.template_file.user_data.rendered}"

  lifecycle {
    create_before_destroy = true
  }
}
```

Now, in the staging environment, in *live/stage/services/webserver-cluster/main.tf*, you can set the new ami and server_text parameters and remove the enable_new_user_data parameter:

```
module "webserver_cluster" {
  source = "../../../../modules/services/webserver-cluster"

  ami         = "ami-40d28157"
  server_text = "New server text"

  cluster_name          = "webservers-stage"
  db_remote_state_bucket = "(YOUR_BUCKET_NAME)"
  db_remote_state_key   = "stage/data-stores/mysql/terraform.tfstate"

  instance_type     = "t2.micro"
  min_size          = 2
  max_size          = 2
  enable_autoscaling = false
}
```

This code uses the same Ubuntu AMI, but changes the server_text to a new value. If you run the plan command, you should see something like the following (I've omitted some of the output for clarity):

```
~ module.webserver_cluster.aws_autoscaling_group.example
    launch_configuration:
      "terraform-2016182624wu" => "${aws_launch_configuration.example.id}"

-/+ module.webserver_cluster.aws_launch_configuration.example
    ebs_block_device.#:  "0" => "<computed>"
    ebs_optimized:       "false" => "<computed>"
    enable_monitoring:   "true" => "true"
    image_id:            "ami-40d28157" => "ami-40d28157"
    instance_type:       "t2.micro" => "t2.micro"
    key_name:            "" => "<computed>"
    name:                "terraform-2016wu" => "<computed>"
    root_block_device.#: "0" => "<computed>"
    security_groups.#:   "1" => "1"
    user_data:           "416115339b" => "3bab6ede8dc" (forces new resource)


Plan: 1 to add, 1 to change, 1 to destroy.
```

As you can see, Terraform wants to make two changes: first, replace the old launch configuration with a new one that has the updated user_data, and second, modify the Auto Scaling Group to reference the new launch configuration. The problem is that merely referencing the new launch configuration will have no effect until the Auto Scaling Group launches new EC2 Instances. So how do you tell the Auto Scaling Group to deploy new Instances?

One option is to destroy the ASG (e.g., by running `terraform destroy`) and then re-create it (e.g., by running `terraform apply`). The problem is that after you delete the old ASG, your users will experience downtime until the new ASG comes up. What you want to do instead is a *zero-downtime deployment*. The way to accomplish that is to create the replacement ASG first and then destroy the original one. As it turns out, this is exactly what the `create_before_destroy` lifecycle setting does!

Here's how you can take advantage of this lifecycle setting to get a zero-downtime deployment:[3]

1. Configure the `name` parameter of the ASG to depend directly on the name of the launch configuration. That way, each time the launch configuration changes (which it will when you update the AMI or User Data), Terraform will try to replace the ASG.

2. Set the `create_before_destroy` parameter of the ASG to `true`, so each time Terraform tries to replace it, it will create the replacement before destroying the original.

3. Set the `min_elb_capacity` parameter of the ASG to the `min_size` of the cluster so that Terraform will wait for at least that many servers from the new ASG to register in the ELB before it'll start destroying the original ASG.

Here is what the updated `aws_autoscaling_group` resource should look like in *modules/services/webserver-cluster/main.tf*:

```
resource "aws_autoscaling_group" "example" {
  name = "${var.cluster_name}-${aws_launch_configuration.example.name}"

  launch_configuration = "${aws_launch_configuration.example.id}"
  availability_zones   = ["${data.aws_availability_zones.all.names}"]
  load_balancers       = ["${aws_elb.example.name}"]
  health_check_type    = "ELB"

  min_size        = "${var.min_size}"
  max_size        = "${var.max_size}"
  min_elb_capacity = "${var.min_size}"

  lifecycle {
    create_before_destroy = true
  }

  tag {
    key                 = "Name"
    value               = "${var.cluster_name}"
    propagate_at_launch = true
```

---

3 Credit for this technique goes to Paul Hinze (*http://bit.ly/2lksQgv*).

```
      }
    }
```

As you may remember, a gotcha with the `create_before_destroy` parameter is that if you set it to `true` on a resource R, you also have to set it to `true` on every resource that R depends on. In the web server cluster module, the `aws_autoscaling_group` resource depends on one other resource, the `aws_elb`. The `aws_elb`, in turn, depends on one other resource, an `aws_security_group`. Set `create_before_destroy` to `true` on both of those resources.

If you rerun the `plan` command, you'll now see something that looks like this (I've omitted some of the output for clarity):

```
-/+ module.webserver_cluster.aws_autoscaling_group.example
    availability_zones.#:      "4" => "4"
    default_cooldown:          "300" => "<computed>"
    desired_capacity:          "2" => "<computed>"
    force_delete:              "false" => "false"
    health_check_type:         "ELB" => "ELB"
    launch_configuration:      "terraform-20161wu" =>
"${aws_launch_configuration.example.id}"
    max_size:                  "2" => "2"
    min_elb_capacity:          "" => "2"
    min_size:                  "2" => "2"
    name:                      "tf-asg-200170wox" => "${var.cluster_name}
-${aws_launch_configuration.example.name}" (forces new resource)
    protect_from_scale_in:     "false" => "false"
    tag.#:                     "1" => "1"
    tag.2305202985.key:        "Name" => "Name"
    tag.2305202985.value:      "webservers-stage" => "webservers-stage"
    vpc_zone_identifier.#:     "1" => "<computed>"
    wait_for_capacity_timeout: "10m" => "10m"

-/+ module.webserver_cluster.aws_launch_configuration.example
    ebs_block_device.#:   "0" => "<computed>"
    ebs_optimized:        "false" => "<computed>"
    enable_monitoring:    "true" => "true"
    image_id:             "ami-40d28157" => "ami-40d28157"
    instance_type:        "t2.micro" => "t2.micro"
    key_name:             "" => "<computed>"
    name:                 "terraform-20161118182404wu" => "<computed>"
    root_block_device.#:  "0" => "<computed>"
    security_groups.#:    "1" => "1"
    user_data:            "416115339b" => "3bab6edc" (forces new resource)

Plan: 2 to add, 2 to change, 2 to destroy.
```

The key thing to notice is that the `aws_autoscaling_group` resource now says "forces new resource" next to its name parameter, which means Terraform will replace it with a new Auto Scaling Group running the new version of your code (or new version of your User Data). Run the `apply` command to kick off the deployment, and while it runs, consider how the process works. You start with your original ASG running, say, v1 of your code (Figure 5-1).

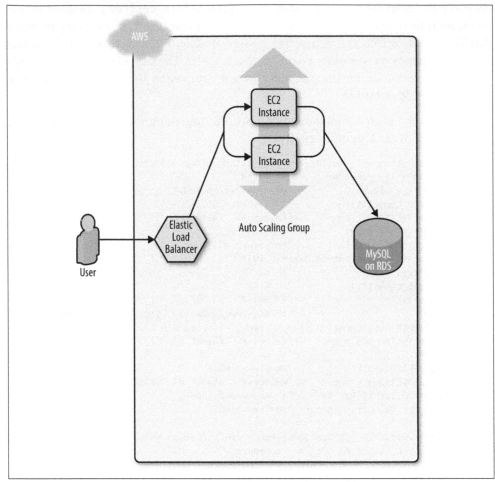

Figure 5-1. Initially, you have the original ASG running v1 of your code

You make an update to some aspect of the launch configuration, such as switching to an AMI that contains v2 of your code, and run the apply command. This forces Terraform to start deploying a new ASG with v2 of your code (Figure 5-2).

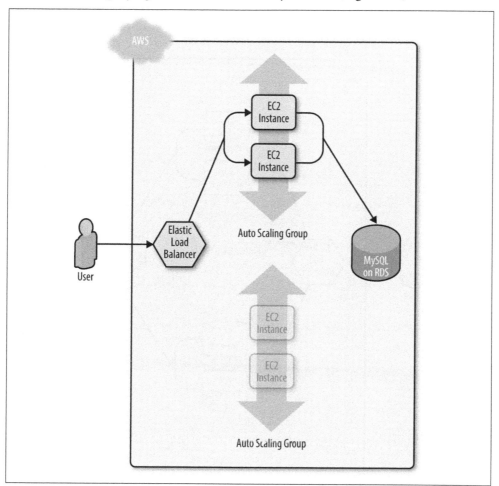

Figure 5-2. Terraform begins deploying the new ASG with v2 of your code

After a minute or two, the servers in the new ASG have booted, connected to the database, and registered in the ELB. At this point, both the v1 and v2 versions of your app will be running simultaneously, and which one users see depends on where the ELB happens to route them (Figure 5-3).

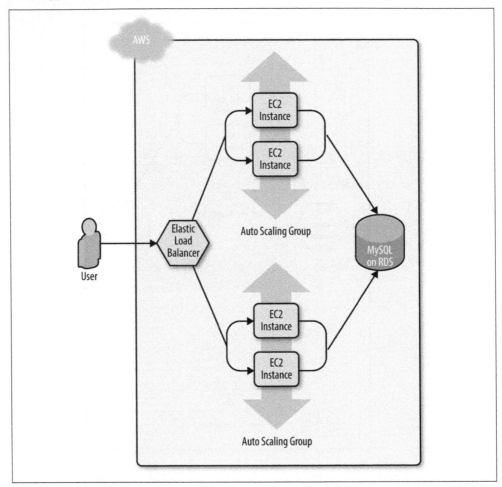

Figure 5-3. The servers in the new ASG boot up, connect to the DB, register in the ELB, and start serving traffic

Once `min_elb_capacity` servers from the v2 ASG cluster have registered in the ELB, Terraform will begin to undeploy the old ASG, first by deregistering the servers in that ASG from the ELB, and then by shutting them down (Figure 5-4).

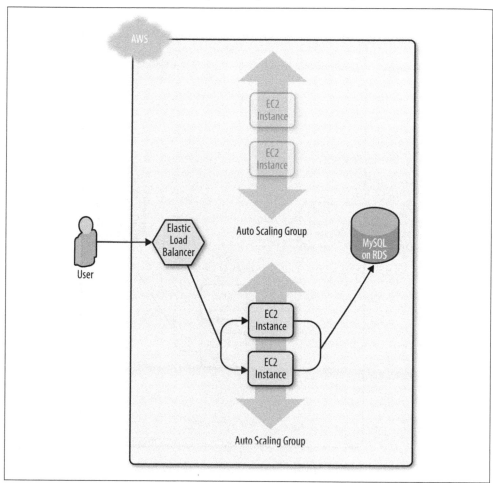

Figure 5-4. *The servers in the old ASG begin to shut down*

After a minute or two, the old ASG will be gone, and you will be left with just v2 of your app running in the new ASG (Figure 5-5).

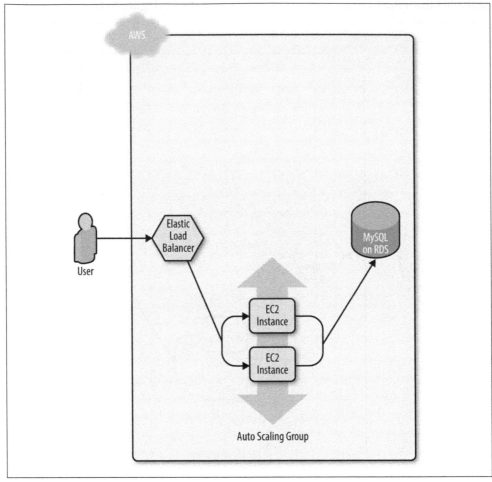

Figure 5-5. Now, only the new ASG remains, which is running v2 of your code

During this entire process, there are always servers running and handling requests from the ELB, so there is no downtime. Open the ELB URL in your browser and you should see something like Figure 5-6.

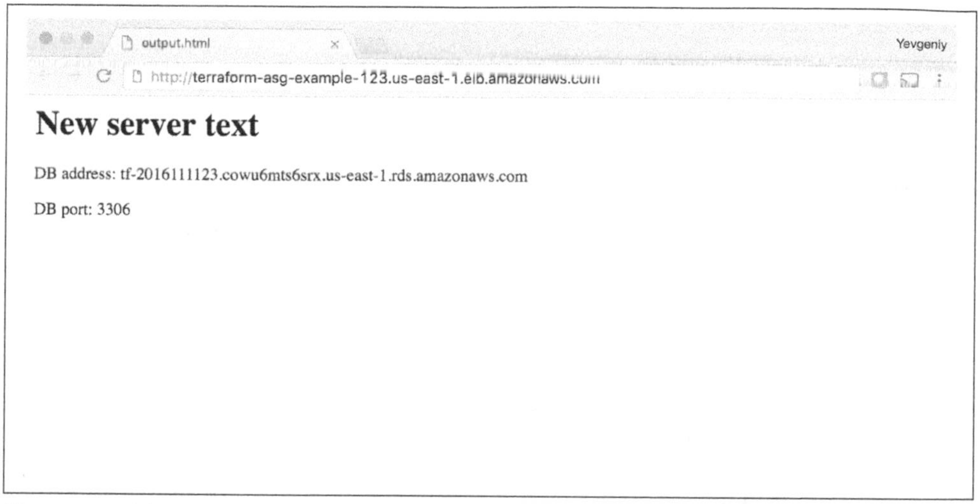

Figure 5-6. The new code is now deployed

Success! The new server text has deployed. As a fun experiment, make another change to the `server_text` parameter (e.g., update it to say "foo bar"), and run the `apply` command. In a separate terminal tab, if you're on Linux/Unix/OS X, you can use a Bash one-liner to run `curl` in a loop, hitting your ELB once per second, and allowing you to see the zero-downtime deployment in action:

```
> while true; do curl http://<load_balancer_url>; sleep 1; done
```

For the first minute or so, you should see the same response that says "New server text". Then, you'll start seeing it alternate between the "New server text" and "foo bar". This means the new Instances have registered in the ELB. After another minute, the "New server text" will disappear, and you'll only see "foo bar", which means the old ASG has been shut down. The output will look something like this (for clarity, I'm listing only the contents of the `<h1>` tags):

```
New server text
New server text
New server text
New server text
New server text
New server text
foo bar
New server text
foo bar
New server text
foo bar
New server text
foo bar
New server text
foo bar
```

```
New server text
foo bar
foo bar
foo bar
foo bar
foo bar
foo bar
```

As an added bonus, if something went wrong during the deployment, Terraform will automatically roll back! For example, if there was a bug in v2 of your app and it failed to boot, then the Instances in the new ASG will not register with the ELB. Terraform will wait up to `wait_for_capacity_timeout` (default is 10 minutes) for `min_elb_capacity` servers of the v2 ASG to register in the ELB, after which it will consider the deployment a failure, delete the v2 ASG, and exit with an error (meanwhile, v1 of your app continues to run just fine in the original ASG).

Terraform Gotchas

After going through all these tips and tricks, it's worth taking a step back and pointing out a few gotchas, including those related to the loop, if-statement, and deployment techniques, as well as those related to more general problems that affect Terraform as a whole:

- Count has limitations
- Zero-downtime deployment has limitations
- Valid plans can fail
- Refactoring can be tricky
- Eventual consistency is consistent…eventually

Count Has Limitations

In the examples in this chapter, you made extensive use of the count parameter in loops and if-statements. This works well, but there is a significant limitation: you cannot use dynamic data in the count parameter. By "dynamic data," I mean any data that is fetched from a provider (e.g., from a data source) or is only available after a resource has been created (e.g., an output attribute of a resource).

For example, imagine you wanted to deploy multiple EC2 Instances, and for some reason did not want to use an Auto Scaling Group to do it. The code might look something like this:

```
resource "aws_instance" "example" {
  count         = 3
  ami           = "ami-40d28157"
```

```
  instance_type = "t2.micro"
}
```

What if you wanted to deploy one EC2 Instance per availability zone (AZ) in the current AWS region? You might be tempted to use the `aws_availability_zones` data source to retrieve the list of AZs and update the code as follows:

```
data "aws_availability_zones" "all" {}

resource "aws_instance" "example" {
  count               = "${length(data.aws_availability_zones.all.names)}"
  availability_zone =
    "${element(data.aws_availability_zones.all.names, count.index)}"

  ami           = "ami-40d28157"
  instance_type = "t2.micro"
}
```

This code uses the `length` interpolation function to set the `count` parameter to the number of available AZs, and the `element` interpolation function with `count.index` to set the `availability_zone` parameter to a different AZ for each EC2 Instance. This is a perfectly reasonable approach, but unfortunately, if you run this code, you'll get an error that looks like this:

```
aws_instance.example:resource count can't reference resource variable:
data.aws_availability_zones.all.names
```

The cause is that Terraform tries to resolve all the count parameters *before* fetching any dynamic data. Therefore, it's trying to parse `${length(data.aws_availabil ity_zones.all.names)}` as a number *before* it has fetched the list of AZs. This is an inherent limitation in Terraform's design and, as of January 2017, it's an open issue (*https://github.com/hashicorp/terraform/issues/3888*) in the Terraform community.

For now, your only option is to manually look up how many AZs you have in your AWS region (every AWS account has access to different AZs, so check your EC2 console (*https://console.aws.amazon.com/ec2*)) and hard-code the `count` parameter to that value:

```
resource "aws_instance" "example" {
  count               = 3
  availability_zone =
    "${element(data.aws_availability_zones.all.names, count.index)}"

  ami           = "ami-40d28157"
  instance_type = "t2.micro"
}
```

Alternatively, you can set the `count` parameter to a variable:

```
resource "aws_instance" "example" {
  count               = "${var.num_availability_zones}"
```

```
  availability_zone =
    "${element(data.aws_availability_zones.all.names, count.index)}"

  ami           = "ami-40d28157"
  instance_type = "t2.micro"
}
```

However, the value for that variable must also be hard-coded somewhere along the line (e.g., via a `default` defined with the variable or a value passed in via the command-line `-var` option) and not depend on any dynamic data:

```
variable "num_availability_zones" {
  description = "The number of Availability Zones in the AWS region"
  default     = 3
}
```

Zero-Downtime Deployment has Limitations

Using `create_before_destroy` with an ASG is a great technique for zero-downtime deployment, but there is one limitation: it doesn't work with auto scaling policies. Or, to be more accurate, it resets your ASG size back to its `min_size` after each deployment, which can be a problem if you had used auto scaling policies to increase the number of running servers.

For example, the web server cluster module includes a couple of `aws_autoscal ing_schedule` resources that increase the number of servers in the cluster from 2 to 10 at 9 a.m. If you ran a deployment at, say, 11 a.m., the replacement ASG would boot up with only 2 servers, rather than 10, and would stay that way until 9 a.m. the next day.

There are several possible workarounds, including:

- Change the `recurrence` parameter on the `aws_autoscaling_schedule` from `0 9 * * *`, which means "run at 9 a.m.", to something like `0-59 9-17 * * *`, which means "run every minute from 9 a.m. to 5 p.m." If the ASG already has 10 servers, rerunning this auto scaling policy will have no effect, which is just fine; and if the ASG was just deployed, then running this policy ensures that the ASG won't be around for more than a minute before the number of Instances is increased to 10. This approach is a bit of a hack, and while it may work for scheduled auto scaling actions, it does not work for auto scaling policies triggered by load (e.g., "add two servers if CPU utilization is over 95%").

- Create a custom script that uses the AWS API to figure out how many servers are running in the ASG before deployment, use that value as the `desired_capacity` parameter of the ASG in the Terraform configurations, and then kick off the deployment. After the new ASG has booted, the script should remove the `desired_capacity` parameter so that the auto scaling policies can control the size of the ASG. On the plus side, the replacement ASG will boot up with the same number of servers as the original, and this approach works with all types of auto scaling policies. The downside is that it requires a custom and somewhat complicated deployment script rather than pure Terraform code.

Ideally, Terraform would have first-class support for zero-downtime deployment, but as of January 2017, this is an open issue (*https://github.com/hashicorp/terraform/ issues/1552*) in the Terraform community.

Valid Plans Can Fail

Sometimes, you run the `plan` command and it shows you a perfectly valid-looking plan, but when you run `apply`, you'll get an error. For example, try to add an `aws_iam_user` resource with the exact same name you used for the IAM user you created in Chapter 2:

```
resource "aws_iam_user" "existing_user" {
  # You should change this to the username of an IAM user that already
  # exists so you can practice using the terraform import command
  name = "yevgeniy.brikman"
}
```

If you now run the `plan` command, Terraform will show you a plan that looks reasonable:

```
+ aws_iam_user.existing_user
    arn:           "<computed>"
    force_destroy: "false"
    name:          "yevgeniy.brikman"
    path:          "/"
    unique_id:     "<computed>"

Plan: 1 to add, 0 to change, 0 to destroy.
```

If you run the `apply` command, you'll get the following error:

```
Error applying plan:

* aws_iam_user.existing_user: Error creating IAM User yevgeniy.brikman:
EntityAlreadyExists: User with name yevgeniy.brikman already exists.
```

The problem, of course, is that an IAM user with that name already exists. This can happen not only with IAM users, but almost any resource. Perhaps someone created it manually or with a different set of Terraform configurations, but either way, some identifier is the same, and that leads to a conflict. There are many variations on this error, and Terraform newbies are often caught offguard by them.

The key realization is that `terraform plan` only looks at resources in its Terraform state file. If you create resources *out-of-band*—such as by manually clicking around the AWS console—they will not be in Terraform's state file, and therefore, Terraform will not take them into account when you run the plan command. As a result, a valid-looking plan may still fail.

There are two main lessons to take away from this:

Once you start using Terraform, you should only use Terraform
> Once a part of your infrastructure is managed by Terraform, you should never make changes manually to it. Otherwise, you not only set yourself up for weird Terraform errors, but you also void many of the benefits of using infrastructure as code in the first place, as that code will no longer be an accurate representation of your infrastructure.

If you have existing infrastructure, use the import command
> If you created infrastructure before you started using Terraform, you can use the terraform import command to add that infrastructure to Terraform's state file, so Terraform is aware of and can manage that infrastructure. The import command takes two arguments. The first argument is the "address" of the resource in your Terraform configuration files. This makes use of the same syntax as interpolations, such as TYPE.NAME (e.g., aws_iam_user.existing_user). The second argument is a resource-specific ID that identifies the resource to import. For example, the ID for an aws_iam_user resource is the name of the user (e.g., yevgeniy.brikman) and the ID for an aws_instance is the EC2 Instance ID (e.g., i-190e22e5). The documentation for each resource typically specifies how to import it at the bottom of the page.

For example, here is the import command you can use to sync the aws_iam_user you just added in your Terraform configurations with the IAM user you created back in Chapter 2 (obviously, you should replace "yevgeniy.brikman" with your own username in this command):

```
> terraform import aws_iam_user.existing_user yevgeniy.brikman
```

Terraform will use the AWS API to find your IAM user and create an association in its state file between that user and the aws_iam_user.existing_user resource in your Terraform configurations. From then on, when you run the plan command, Terraform will know that IAM user already exists and not try to create it again.

Note that if you have a lot of existing resources that you want to import into Terraform, writing the Terraform code for them from scratch and importing them one at a time can be painful, so you may want to look into a tool such as Terraforming (*http://terraforming.dtan4.net/*), which can import both code and state from an AWS account automatically.

Refactoring Can Be Tricky

A common programming practice is *refactoring*, where you restructure the internal details of an existing piece of code without changing its external behavior. The goal is to improve the readability, maintainability, and general hygiene of the code. Refactoring is an essential coding practice that you should do regularly. However, when it comes to Terraform, or any infrastructure as code tool, you have to be careful about what defines the "external behavior" of a piece of code, or you will run into unexpected problems.

For example, a common refactoring practice is to rename a variable or a function to give it a clearer name. Many IDEs even have built-in support for refactoring and can rename the variable or function for you, automatically, across the entire codebase. While such a renaming is something you might do without thinking twice in a general-purpose programming language, you have to be very careful in how you do it in Terraform, or it could lead to an outage.

For example, the `webserver-cluster` module has an input variable named `cluster_name`:

```
variable "cluster_name" {
  description = "The name to use for all the cluster resources"
}
```

Perhaps you start using this module for deploying microservices, and initially, you set your microservice's name to `foo`. Later on, you decide you want to rename the service to `bar`. This may seem like a trivial change, but it may actually cause an outage.

That's because the `webserver-cluster` module uses the `cluster_name` variable in a number of resources, including the `name` parameters of the ELB and two security groups. If you change the `name` parameter of certain resources, Terraform will delete the old version of the resource and create a new version to replace it. If the resource you are deleting happens to be an ELB, there will be nothing to route traffic to your web server cluster until the new ELB boots up. Similarly, if the resource you are deleting happens to be a security group, your servers will reject all network traffic until the new security group is created.

Another refactor you may be tempted to do is to change a Terraform identifier. For example, consider the `aws_security_group` resource in the `webserver-cluster` module:

```
resource "aws_security_group" "instance" {
  name = "${var.cluster_name}-instance"

  lifecycle {
    create_before_destroy = true
  }
}
```

The identifier for this resource is called `instance`. Perhaps you were doing a refactor and you thought it would be clearer to change this name to `cluster_instance`. What's the result? Yup, you guessed it: downtime.

Terraform associates each resource identifier with an identifier from the cloud provider, such as associating an `iam_user` resource with an AWS IAM User ID or an `aws_instance` resource with an AWS EC2 Instance ID. If you change the resource identifier, such as changing the `aws_security_group` identifier from `instance` to `cluster_instance`, then as far as Terraform knows, you deleted the old resource and have added a completely new one. As a result, if you `apply` these changes, Terraform will delete the old security group and create a new one, and in the time period in between, your servers will reject all network traffic.

There are four main lessons you should take away from this discussion:

Always use the plan command

> All of these gotchas can be caught by running the `plan` command, carefully scanning the output, and noticing that Terraform plans to delete a resource that you probably don't want deleted.

Create before destroy

> If you do want to replace a resource, then think carefully about whether its replacement should be created before you delete the original. If so, then you may be able to use `create_before_destroy` to make that happen. Alternatively, you can also accomplish the same effect through two manual steps: first, add the new resource to your configurations and run the `apply` command; second, remove the old resource from your configurations and run the `apply` command again.

All identifiers are immutable

> Treat the identifiers you associate with each resource as immutable. If you change an identifier, Terraform will delete the old resource and create a new one to replace it. Therefore, don't rename identifiers unless absolutely necessary, and even then, use the `plan` command, and consider whether you should use a create-before-destroy strategy.

Some parameters are immutable

> The parameters of many resources are immutable, so if you change them, Terraform will delete the old resource and create a new one to replace it. The documentation for each resource often specifies what happens if you change a parameter, so RTFM. And, once again, make sure to always use the `plan` command, and consider whether you should use a create-before-destroy strategy.

Eventual Consistency Is Consistent…Eventually

The APIs for some cloud providers, such as AWS, are asynchronous and eventually consistent. *Asynchronous* means the API may send a response immediately, without waiting for the requested action to complete. *Eventually consistent* means it takes time for a change to propagate throughout the entire system, so for some period of time, you may get inconsistent responses depending on which data store replica happens to respond to your API calls.

For example, let's say you make an API call to AWS asking it to create an EC2 Instance. The API will return a "success" (i.e., 201 Created) response more or less instantly, without waiting for the EC2 Instance creation to complete. If you tried to connect to that EC2 Instance immediately, you'd most likely fail because AWS is still provisioning it or the Instance hasn't booted yet. Moreover, if you made another API call to fetch information about that EC2 Instance, you may get an error in return (i.e., 404 Not Found). That's because the information about that EC2 Instance may still be propagating throughout AWS, and it'll take a few seconds before it's available everywhere.

In short, whenever you use an asynchronous and eventually consistent API, you are supposed to wait and retry for a while until that action has completed and propagated. Unfortunately, Terraform does not do a great job of this. As of version 0.8.x, Terraform still has a number of eventual consistency bugs that you will hit from time to time after running `terraform apply`.

For example, there is #5335 (*https://github.com/hashicorp/terraform/issues/5335*):

```
> terraform apply
aws_route.internet-gateway:
error finding matching route for Route table (rtb-5ca64f3b)
and destination CIDR block (0.0.0.0/0)
```

And #5185 (*https://github.com/hashicorp/terraform/issues/5185*):

```
> terraform apply
Resource 'aws_eip.nat' does not have attribute 'id' for variable 'aws_eip.nat.id'
```

And #6813 (*https://github.com/hashicorp/terraform/issues/6813*):

```
> terraform apply
aws_subnet.private-persistence.2: InvalidSubnetID.NotFound:
The subnet ID 'subnet-xxxxxxx' does not exist
```

These bugs are annoying, but fortunately, most of them are harmless. If you just rerun `terraform apply`, everything will work fine, since by the time you rerun it, the information has propagated throughout the system.

It's also worth noting that eventual consistency bugs may be more likely if the place from where you're running Terraform is geographically far away from the provider you're using. For example, if you're running Terraform on your laptop in California and you're deploying code to the AWS region `eu-west-1`, which is thousands of miles away in Ireland, you are more likely to see eventual consistency bugs. I'm guessing this is because the API calls from Terraform get routed to a local AWS data center (e.g., `us-west-1`, which is in California), and the replicas in that data center take a longer time to update if the actual changes are happening in a different data center.

Conclusion

Although Terraform is a declarative language, it includes a large number of tools, such as variables and modules, which you saw in Chapter 4, and `count`, `create_before_destroy`, and interpolation functions, which you saw in this chapter, that give the language a surprising amount of flexibility and expressive power. There are many permutations of the if-statement tricks shown in this chapter, so spend some time browsing the interpolation documentation (*https://www.terraform.io/docs/ configuration/interpolation.html*) and let your inner hacker go wild. OK, maybe not too wild, as someone still has to maintain your code, but just wild enough that you can create clean, beautiful APIs for your users.

These users will be the focus of the next chapter, which describes how to use Terraform as a team. This includes a discussion of what workflows you can use, how to manage environments, how to test your Terraform configurations, and more.

## CHAPTER 6

How to Use Terraform as a Team

If your team is used to managing all of its infrastructure by hand, switching to infrastructure as code (IAC) requires more than just introducing a new tool or technology. It also requires changing the culture and processes of the team. In particular, your team will need to shift from a mindset of making changes directly to infrastructure (e.g., by SSHing to a server and running commands) to a mindset where you make those changes indirectly (e.g., by updating Terraform code) and allowing automated processes to do all the actual work.

Making this transition can be a bit uncomfortable. Initially, team members may complain, as learning new languages, new technologies, and new processes will feel slower and more complicated than just jumping onto a server manually like they've been doing for years. But this up-front investment in learning has a massive payoff. Doing things by hand may feel simpler and faster for a few servers, but once you have tens, hundreds, or thousands of servers, proper IAC processes are the only options that work.

In this chapter, I'll dive into the key processes you need to put in place to make IAC work for your team, including:

- Version control
- Automated testing
- Coding guidelines
- Workflow

Let's go through these topics one at a time.

Version Control

All of your code should be in version control. No exceptions. It was the #1 item on the classic Joel Test (*http://bit.ly/2meqAb7*) when Joel Spolsky created it 16+ years ago, and the only things that have changed since then are that (a) with tools like GitHub, it's easier than ever to use version control and (b) you can represent more and more things as code. This includes documentation (e.g., a README written in Markdown), application configuration (e.g., a config file written in YAML), specifications (e.g., test code written with RSpec), tests (e.g., automated tests written with JUnit), databases (e.g., schema migrations written in Active Record), and of course, infrastructure.

Not only should the code that defines your infrastructure be stored in version control, but you may want to have at least two separate version control repositories: one for modules, and one for live infrastructure. Let's look at these one at a time.

A Repository for Modules

As discussed in Chapter 4, your team should have one or more separate repositories where you define versioned, reusable modules. Think of each module as a "blueprint" that defines a specific part of your infrastructure.

The beauty of this arrangement is that you could have an infrastructure team that specializes in creating reusable, best-practices definitions of pieces of infrastructure within the *modules* repo. For example, the infrastructure team could take the `webserver-cluster` module you've developed in this book and turn it into a canonical module everyone at your company can use to run their microservices. This module handles all the details of deployment, scaling, load balancing, monitoring, alerting, and so on, so all of the other dev teams can grab this module and create and manage their own microservices independently, without being bottlenecked by the infrastructure team.

A Repository for Live Infrastructure

There should be a separate repository that defines the live infrastructure you're running in each environment (stage, prod, mgmt, etc). Think of this as the "houses" you build from the "blueprints" in the *modules* repository. For example, here is how a dev team might use the microservice module to deploy a search and a profile microservice with different settings for each one:

```
module "search_service" {
  source = "../../../../modules/services/webserver-cluster"

  ami         = "${data.aws_ami.ubuntu.id}"
  server_text = "Hello from search"

  cluster_name          = "search-service-prod"
  db_remote_state_bucket = "(YOUR_BUCKET_NAME)"
  db_remote_state_key    = "prod/data-stores/mysql/terraform.tfstate"

  instance_type = "x1.16xlarge"
  min_size      = 4
  max_size      = 4

  enable_autoscaling = false
}
module "profile_service" {
  source = "../../../../modules/services/webserver-cluster"

  ami         = "${data.aws_ami.ubuntu.id}"
  server_text = "Hello from profile"

  cluster_name          = "profile-service-prod"
  db_remote_state_bucket = "(YOUR_BUCKET_NAME)"
  db_remote_state_key    = "prod/data-stores/mysql/terraform.tfstate"

  instance_type = "m4.large"
  min_size      = 12
  max_size      = 40

  enable_autoscaling = true
}
```

Since everyone is using the same "canonical" modules under the hood, and since those modules are versioned (which is possible because those modules are defined in a separate repository), the infrastructure team can ensure that even as the company and the number of microservices grows, everything remains consistent and maintainable. Or to be more accurate, it will remain maintainable as long as you follow the golden rule of Terraform.

The Golden Rule of Terraform

You should be able to reason about your infrastructure just by looking at the live repository. If you can scan the code of that repository and get an accurate understanding of what's deployed, then you'll find it easy to maintain your infrastructure. If you have to resort to checking a web console, or worse yet, relying on your developers to remember what they did or why they did it, you will find maintenance much more difficult.

This idea can be captured in a single sentence that I shall dub *The Golden Rule of Terraform*:

> The master branch of the live repository should be a 1:1 representation of what's actually deployed in production.

Let's break this sentence down, starting at the end and working our way back:

"…what's actually deployed"

The only way to ensure that the Terraform code in the live repository is an up-to-date representation of what's actually deployed is to *never make out-of-band changes*. Once you start using Terraform, do not make changes via a web UI, or manual API calls, or any other mechanism. As you saw in Chapter 5, out-of-band changes not only lead to complicated bugs, but they also void many of the benefits you get from using infrastructure as code in the first place.

"…a 1:1 representation…"

Every resource you have deployed should have a corresponding line of code in your live repository. This may seem obvious, but as a Terraform newbie, you may be tempted to "reuse" the same set of Terraform configurations to deploy many resources. For example, you might define a single set of configuration files to deploy a server, and then try to create 10 servers by running `terraform apply` 10 times on this same set of configuration files, configuring it to use a different state file and passing in different parameters via the `-var` options each time. If you do this, then after reading through the Terraform code, you'll still have no idea what's actually deployed, as the code gives no indication whether you ran `terraform apply` once or 10 times. The better way to get this kind of reuse is to create a module, write explicit code that uses that module 10 times, and run `terraform apply` once. Alternatively, you can use the same set of configurations over and over again, but you should store the unique variables and remote state configuration in files (you'll see an example of this in "Larger Teams May Need to Use a Development Pipeline" on page 163).

"The master branch…"

You should only have to look at a single branch to understand what's actually deployed in production. Typically, that branch will be master. That means all changes that affect the production environment should go directly into master (you can create a separate branch, but only to create a pull request with the intention of merging that branch into master) and you should only run `terraform apply` for the production environment against the master branch. I'll discuss the process of making changes in master and in production in "Workflow" on page 157.

Automated Tests

When you manage infrastructure manually, every time you go to make a change, there is an element of fear and uncertainty. You're not sure exactly what that change will affect or if it'll work the way you expect. You're not sure if you applied the change the same way on all servers in all environments. You're not sure if there will be another outage, and if there is, how late into the night you'll have to work to fix it. As companies grow, there is more and more at stake, which makes the manual deployment process even scarier, and even more error prone. Many companies try to mitigate this risk by doing deployments less frequently, but the result is that each deployment is larger, and actually more prone to breakage.

If you manage your infrastructure through code, you have a better way to mitigate risk: automated tests. The idea is to write code that verifies that your infrastructure code works as expected. You should run these tests after every commit and revert any commits that fail. This way, every change that makes it into your codebase is proven to work and most issues will be found at build time rather than during a nervewracking deployment.

How do you write automated tests for Terraform configurations? Here are the steps:

- Prepare your code
- Write the test code
- Use multiple types of automated tests

Prepare Your Code

One of the challenges with testing Terraform code is that, under the hood, Terraform configurations are just a convenient language for making API calls to a provider (e.g., making API calls to AWS). With automated tests for general-purpose programming languages, you'd often replace complicated dependencies, such as AWS, with *test doubles*, which implement the API of the dependency, but return hard-coded data that's convenient for testing. With automated tests for Terraform, this technique isn't as useful, as the interaction with that complicated dependency (such as AWS) is precisely what you want to test!

Therefore, most automated tests for Terraform simply run `terraform apply` and then try to verify that the deployed resources behave as expected. That means that automated tests for infrastructure are a bit slower to run and a bit more fragile than other types of automated tests. However, this is a small price to pay for the ability to validate all your infrastructure changes before those changes can cause problems in production. Let's go through an example.

At the end of Chapter 5, you were deploying a web server cluster in the production environment as follows:

```
provider "aws" {
  region = "us-east-1"
}

module "webserver_cluster" {
  source = "../../../../modules/services/webserver-cluster"

  ami         = "ami-40d28157"
  server_text = "Hello, World"

  cluster_name          = "webservers-prod"
  db_remote_state_bucket = "(YOUR_BUCKET_NAME)"
  db_remote_state_key   = "prod/data-stores/mysql/terraform.tfstate"

  instance_type     = "m4.large"
  min_size          = 2
  max_size          = 10
  enable_autoscaling = true
}
```

How can you write an automated test that verifies if this cluster works? Ideally, you would deploy the cluster into an isolated environment and test that when you hit the ELB URL, it returns the text you expect. However, if you wrote an automated test that ran `terraform apply` directly on this code, you'd run into a problem: the code is designed for deployment into the production environment, so your automated test would run in production, too, which could cause problems!

To avoid these problems, you need to make it possible to deploy your Terraform configurations into an isolated test environment by making the following parameters configurable:

region

> The `aws` provider is hard-coded to the `us-east-1` region. It can be risky to run arbitrary test code (which could have its own bugs!) in the same region as you run your production code, so you'll need a way to specify a custom region that is dedicated for testing and has no chance of affecting production.[1]

cluster_name

> The `cluster_name` parameter is hard-coded to `"webservers-prod"`. This `clus ter_name` parameter is used as the name of all the resources created by the

---

[1] You may want to run tests not only in an isolated region, but also an isolated Virtual Private Cloud (VPC) within that region. All the code in this book uses the Default VPC to keep the examples simple, but in real-world use cases, you should explicitly specify a VPC for staging, production, and test, and ensure that all three are completely isolated from each other.

webserver-cluster module, including the names of the ELB and security groups. The problem is that these names must be unique, so if someone else has deployed the same web server cluster in the same region (e.g., another developer on your team running the same test at the same time), you'll get an error.

db_remote_state_key

> The db_remote_state_key is hard-coded to "prod/data-stores/mysql/terra form.tfstate", which is the production database. You definitely don't want to run any automated tests against it, so you need a way to change this value at test time.

Therefore, the first step to making Terraform code testable is to make the various aspects of the environment pluggable. You already know how to do this: use input variables! First, you need to update the webserver-cluster module. Open up *modules/services/webserver-cluster/vars.tf* and add a new input variable for the AWS region:

```
variable "aws_region" {
  description = "The AWS region to use"
}
```

Make use of the new aws_region input variable in *modules/services/webserver-cluster/main.tf* to configure the region parameter of the terraform_remote_state data source:

```
data "terraform_remote_state" "db" {
  backend = "s3"

  config {
    bucket = "${var.db_remote_state_bucket}"
    key    = "${var.db_remote_state_key}"
    region = "${var.aws_region}"
  }
}
```

Next, head back to the production configurations and add four new input variables in *live/prod/services/webserver-cluster/vars.tf* (you should make analogous changes in staging, too):

```
variable "aws_region" {
  description = "The AWS region to use"
  default     = "us-east-1"
}

variable "cluster_name" {
  description = "The name to use for all the cluster resources"
  default     = "webservers-prod"
}

variable "db_remote_state_bucket" {
```

```
    description = "The S3 bucket used for the database's remote state"
    default     = "(YOUR_BUCKET_NAME)"
}

variable "db_remote_state_key" {
  description = "The path for the database's remote state in S3"
  default     = "prod/data-stores/mysql/terraform.tfstate"
}
```

Note that since the AWS region is now configurable, you'll have to update how you specify Amazon Machine Images (AMIs), as the AMI IDs are different in each region. Currently, the `ami` parameter is hard-coded to the ID of an Ubuntu AMI in us-east-1, but the ID of that AMI in another region will be completely different. To figure out the right AMI for each region, you can use the `aws_ami` data source, which allows you to search and filter the AWS Marketplace for a specific AMI. For example, here is how you can find the most recent Ubuntu 16.04 AMI from Canonical:

```
data "aws_ami" "ubuntu" {
  most_recent = true
  owners      = ["099720109477"] # Canonical

  filter {
    name   = "virtualization-type"
    values = ["hvm"]
  }

  filter {
    name   = "architecture"
    values = ["x86_64"]
  }

  filter {
    name   = "image-type"
    values = ["machine"]
  }

  filter {
    name   = "name"
    values = ["ubuntu/images/hvm-ssd/ubuntu-xenial-16.04-amd64-server-*"]
  }
}
```

Pass the `id` output attribute of the `aws_ami` data source, as well as the new input variables, as parameters to the `webserver-cluster` module in *live/prod/services/webserver-cluster/main.tf*:

```
module "webserver_cluster" {
  source = "../../../../modules/services/webserver-cluster"

  ami         = "${data.aws_ami.ubuntu.id}"
  server_text = "Hello, World"
```

```
    aws_region              = "${var.aws_region}"
    cluster_name            = "${var.cluster_name}"
    db_remote_state_bucket = "${var.db_remote_state_bucket}"
    db_remote_state_key     = "${var.db_remote_state_key}"

    instance_type      = "m4.large"
    min_size           = 2
    max_size           = 10
    enable_autoscaling = true
}
```

Also, don't forget to update the `provider` in the same file so it uses the `aws_region` input variable:

```
provider "aws" {
  region = "${var.aws_region}"
}
```

Note how the new input variables set their `default` parameters to the original, hard-coded values so that the behavior of this cluster is exactly the same as it was before. However, by exposing these as variables, you have the *option* to override these values when necessary, such as at test time. In fact, most of these changes have made the code more flexible and powerful. For example, you can now deploy a web server cluster in any AWS region and not just `us-east-1` and it will always use the latest Ubuntu 16.04 release in that region, with all the latest security patches, rather than being fixed to one version forever. This is a common pattern with automated tests: making the code more testable often improves the design of the code overall.

Write the Test Code

Now that you've prepared your Terraform code, you can finally write the actual test code. The test code will need to execute the following steps:

1. Run `terraform apply` on these configurations, passing in values for `cluster_name`, `region`, and `db_remote_state_key` that allow the test to run in complete isolation. For the `cluster_name` variable, you can generate a unique identifier each time the test runs.[2] For the `region` variable, you could pick a region that you don't normally use in production and dedicate it to testing. For the `db_remote_state_key`, you could have a dedicated database for testing or even deploy a mock database each time you run the test.

2. Run the `terraform output` command to retrieve the `elb_dns_name` output.

---

2 For an example of how to generate alphanumeric strings that are unique enough to avoid conflicts and short enough to use as AWS identifiers, see: *http://stackoverflow.com/a/9543797/483528*.

3. Use an HTTP client to test the URL http://<elb_dns_name> and check that the value you get back is what you expect (e.g., "Hello, World"). You may have to retry the HTTP request several times, as the EC2 Instances may take a minute or two to boot up and register in the ELB.

4. Run terraform destroy to clean up all the resources once the test is done.

Here's a simple Ruby script that implements all of these steps:

```ruby
require 'net/http'

if ARGV.length != 3
  raise 'Invalid args. Usage: terraform-test.rb REGION DB_BUCKET DB_KEY'
end

vars = {
    # A unique (ish) 6-char string: http://stackoverflow.com/a/88341/483528
    :cluster_name => (0...6).map { (65 + rand(26)).chr }.join,
    :aws_region => ARGV[0],
    :db_remote_state_bucket => ARGV[1],
    :db_remote_state_key => ARGV[2],
}
vars_string = vars.map{|key, value| "-var '#{key} = \"#{value}\"'"}.join(', ')

def test_url(url, expected_text, retries)
  retries.times do
    begin
      output = Net::HTTP.get(URI.parse(url))
      puts "Output from #{url}: #{output}"
      return 'Success!' if output.include? expected_text
    rescue => e
      puts "Error from #{url}: #{e}"
    end

    puts 'Sleeping for 30 seconds and trying again'
    sleep 30
  end

  raise "Response didn't contain '#{expected_text}' after #{retries} retries"
end

begin
  puts "Deploying code in #{Dir.pwd}"
  puts `terraform get 2>&1`
  puts `terraform apply #{vars_string} 2>&1`

  elb_dns_name = `terraform output -no-color elb_dns_name`
  puts test_url("http://#{elb_dns_name.strip}/", 'Hello, World', 10)
ensure
  puts "Undeploying code in #{Dir.pwd}"
  puts `terraform destroy -force #{vars_string} 2>&1`
end
```

To run the script, you would pick a region for testing (e.g., eu-west-1), deploy some sort of mock database, taking care to remember the S3 bucket name and key used for the database's remote state (e.g., my-terraform-state and test/data-stores/ mysql/terraform.tfstate), and then run:

```
> cd live/prod/services/webserver-cluster
> ruby terraform-test.rb \
    eu-west-1 \
    my-terraform-state \
    test/data-stores/mysql/terraform.tfstate
```

The Ruby script is just a starting point and needs a fair amount of work to make it robust. As an exercise for the reader, I recommend picking your favorite programming language and creating a simple *Domain Specific Language* (DSL) on top of it that gives you reusable primitives for writing automated tests. This DSL could include helper functions for common test tasks, such as running Terraform commands (e.g., apply, output, destroy), verifying HTTP endpoints, and connecting to servers over SSH. You may find some of the existing infrastructure testing tools handy, such as kitchen-terraform (*https://github.com/newcontext-oss/kitchen-terraform*) and server-spec (*http://serverspec.org/*).

Use Multiple Types of Automated Tests

There are several different types of automated tests you may write for your Terraform code, including unit tests, integration tests, and smoke tests. Most teams should use a combination of all three types of tests, as each type can help prevent different types of bugs.

Unit tests

Unit tests verify the functionality of a single, small unit of code. The definition of *unit* varies, but in a general-purpose programming language, it's typically a single function or class. The equivalent in Terraform is to test a single module. For example, if you had a module that deployed a database, then you may want to add tests that run each time someone modifies this module to verify that you can successfully run terraform apply on it, that the database boots successfully after running terraform apply, that you can communicate with the database and store data in it, and so on.

Integration tests

Integration tests verify that multiple units work together correctly. In a general-purpose programming language, you might test that several functions or classes work together correctly. The equivalent in Terraform is to test that several modules work together. For example, let's say you have code in your "live" repo that combines one module that creates a database, another module that creates a cluster of web servers, and a third module that deploys a load balancer. You may want to add integration tests to this repo that run after every commit to verify that `terraform apply` completes without errors, that the database, web server cluster, and load balancer all boot correctly, that you can talk to the web servers via the load balancer, and that the data that comes back is coming from the database.

Smoke tests

Smoke tests run as part of the deployment process, rather than after each commit. You typically have a set of smoke tests that run each time you deploy to staging and production that do a sanity check that the code is working as expected. For example, when an app is booting, the app might run a quick smoke test to ensure it can talk to the database and that it is able to receive HTTP requests. If either of these checks fails, the app can abort the entire deployment before it causes any problems.

Coding Guidelines

Whenever you're writing code as a team, regardless of what type of code you're writing, you should define guidelines for everyone to follow. One of my favorite definitions of "clean code" comes from an interview with Nick Dellamaggiore in the book *Hello, Startup* (*http://www.hello-startup.net*):

> If I look at a single file and it's written by 10 different engineers, it should be almost indistinguishable which part was written by which person. To me, that is clean code.
>
> The way you do that is through code reviews and publishing your style guide, your patterns, and your language idioms. Once you learn them, everybody is way more productive because you all know how to write code the same way. At that point, it's more about what you're writing and not how you write it.
>
> —Nick Dellamaggiore, Infrastructure Lead at Coursera

The coding guidelines that make sense for each team will be different, so here, I'll list a few of the key guidelines to consider and some examples of what you can do for each one:

- Documentation
- File layout
- Style guide

Documentation

In some sense, Terraform code is, in and of itself, a form of documentation. It describes in a simple language exactly what infrastructure you deployed and how that infrastructure is configured. However, there is no such thing as self-documenting code. While well-written code can tell you *what* it does, no programming language I'm aware of (including Terraform) can tell you *why* it does it.

This is why all software, including IAC, needs documentation beyond the code itself. There are several types of documentation you can consider:

Written documentation
> Most Terraform modules should have a Readme that explains what the module does, why it exists, how to use it, and how to modify it. In fact, you may want to write the Readme first, before any of the actual Terraform code, as that will force you to consider *what* you're building and *why* you're building it before you dive into the code and get lost in the details of *how* to build it.[3] Spending 20 minutes writing a Readme can often save you hours of writing code that solves the wrong problem. Beyond the basics of a Readme, you may also want to have tutorials, API documentation, wiki pages, and design documents that go deeper into how the code works and why it was built this way.

Code documentation
> Within the code itself, you can use comments as a form of documentation. Terraform treats any text that starts with a hash (#) as a comment. Don't use comments to explain what the code does; the code should do that itself. Only include comments to offer information that can't be expressed in code, such as how the code is meant to be used or why the code uses a particular design choice. Terraform also allows every input variable to declare a `description` parameter, which is a great place to describe how that variable should be used.

Example code
> When creating Terraform modules, you may also want to create example code that shows how that module is meant to be used. This is a great way to highlight proper usage patterns as well as a way for users to try your module without having to write code. Example code can also be a great place to add automated tests.

File Layout

Your team should define conventions for where Terraform code is stored and the file layout you use. Since the file layout for Terraform also determines the way Terraform state is stored, you should be especially mindful of how file layout impacts your ability to provide isolation guarantees, such as ensuring changes in a staging environment cannot accidentally cause problems in production.

---

3 Writing the Readme first is often called Readme Driven Development, as described here: *http://bit.ly/1p8QBor*.

Take a look at "File Layout" on page 70 for a recommended file layout that provides isolation between different environments (e.g., stage and prod) and different components (e.g., a network topology for the entire environment and a single app within that environment). For larger teams, you may prefer the file layout described later in this chapter in "Larger Teams May Need to Use a Development Pipeline" on page 163.

Note that the file layout for modules is more flexible, since the modules represent reusable code and are not deployed directly. Figure 6-1 shows an example file layout for a module that includes documentation, examples, and test code.

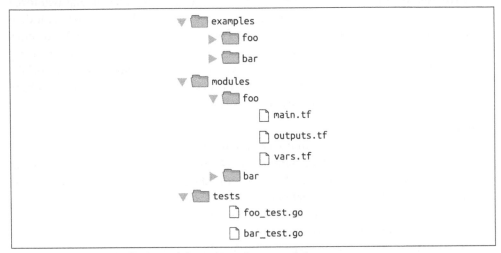

Figure 6-1. Example file layout for a Terraform module

Style Guide

Every team should enforce a set of conventions about code style, including the use of whitespace, newlines, indentation, curly braces, variable naming, and so on. Although programmers love to debate spaces versus tabs and where the curly brace should go, the actual choice isn't that important. What really matters is that you are consistent throughout your codebase. Formatting tools are available for most text editors and IDEs, and as commit hooks for version control systems to help you enforce a common code layout.

Terraform even has a built-in `fmt` command that can reformat code to a consistent style automatically:

```
> terraform fmt
```

You could run this command as part of a commit hook to ensure that all code committed to version control automatically gets a consistent style.

Workflow

Now that you have guidelines for how to write, test, and version Terraform code, the final thing you need is a workflow for making changes to that code. The workflow I recommend for most teams consists of the following:

1. Plan
2. Staging
3. Code review
4. Production

Plan

The `terraform plan` command allows you to see what changes Terraform will make before you actually `apply` those changes. The rule here is simple:

Always run plan before apply.

You'd be amazed at the type of errors you can catch by taking 30 seconds to run this command and scanning the "diff" you get as an output. The `plan` command even allows you to store that diff output in a file:

```
> terraform plan -out=example.plan
```

You can then run the `apply` command on this saved plan file to ensure that it applies *exactly* the changes you saw originally:

```
> terraform apply example.plan
```

Note that, just like Terraform state, the saved plan files may contain secrets. For example, if you're deploying a database with Terraform, the plan file may contain the database password. Since the plan files are not encrypted, if you want to store them for any length of time, you'll have to provide your own encryption.

Once you have a plan that looks good, the next step is to try it out in staging.

Staging

I recommend that every team maintains at least two environments:

Production
    An environment for production workloads (i.e., user-facing apps).

Staging
    An environment for nonproduction workloads (i.e., testing).

Generally, staging should be an exact mirror of production, except perhaps scaled down to save money (i.e., a smaller number of servers and a smaller size for each server).

The rule here is also simple:

> *Always test Terraform changes in staging before production.*

Since everything is automated with Terraform anyway, it doesn't cost you much extra effort to try a change in staging before production, but it will catch a huge number of errors. Note: you have to take into consideration what happens if multiple team members are testing uncommitted changes in staging simultaneously, something I'll come back to later in this chapter.

Testing in staging is especially important because *Terraform does not roll back changes in the case of errors*. If you run `terraform apply` and something goes wrong, you have to fix it yourself. This is easier and less stressful to do if you catch the error in staging rather than production.

If the changes work well in staging, make the same changes to the production code (but do not apply them yet!), and submit a code review.

Code Review

If you're using GitHub, you can submit your changes for a code review using a *pull request*. For other version control systems, you may need to use other code review tools such as Phabricator or ReviewBoard. The code review should include:

Diff output
> Just about every code review tool automatically includes the code diff so everyone can review it. Often, the mere knowledge that someone else will be looking at your code is enough motivation to get you to clean up your code, add more documentation, and write more tests. Even reviewing your own code before committing will often reveal bugs, so it's worth doing a code review even if no one but you actually looks at it!

Plan output
> Run the `plan` command against the production environment and copy/paste the diff it returns into the code review so your teammates can review that, too, and call out anything that looks suspicious.

Automated test output
> If you have automated tests for your Terraform configurations, run them, and paste the output into the code review. If you're using continuous integration tools such as CircleCI, TravisCI, or Jenkins, you can configure them to run after every commit and show the test results in the code review automatically.

The other members on your team should review the code to make sure it follows the coding guidelines from earlier in this chapter. Is the code formatted correctly? Is there example code? Are there automated tests? Has the documentation been updated? Does the plan indicate any possible downtime?

If everything looks good, merge the code into the master branch and prepare for deployment to production.

Production

Once the code has been merged into master, it is safe to deploy to production. As always, run the `plan` command before `apply`, and make sure the plan matches up with what you saw in staging. If everything looks good, run `apply`, and your changes will be live.

This workflow should work for most use cases, but there are three caveats to be aware of that can significantly affect the workflow:

- Some types of Terraform changes can be automated
- Some types of Terraform changes can cause conflicts
- Larger teams may need to use a deployment pipeline

Let's discuss each of these caveats next.

Some Types of Terraform Changes Can Be Automated

The workflow I've outlined works well for infrequent changes, such as adding new infrastructure or reconfiguring existing infrastructure. However, if you're using Terraform to apply the same type of change over and over again, you may want to completely automate the process.

A common use case is to use Terraform to deploy a new version of your app. For example, let's say you have a simple Terraform configuration that deploys an EC2 Instance:

```
resource "aws_instance" "example" {
  ami           = "${var.version}"
  instance_type = "t2.micro"
}
```

The ID of the AMI to deploy is configured via an input variable called `version`:

```
variable "version" {
  description = "The version of the app to deploy"
  default     = "ami-40d28157"
}
```

Every time you deploy a new version of this app, you update the `default` parameter of `var.version` to the new AMI ID, and run `terraform apply`. If you deploy new versions of your app often (e.g., some teams deploy dozens of times per day), doing a code review each time for such a trivial change is too much overhead.

For these sorts of repetitive, mechanical changes, you can write a deployment script that automatically performs the following steps:

1. Check out the live Terraform repository.
2. Update the version number for the app in the corresponding Terraform configurations.
3. Commit the changes back to version control.
4. Run `terraform apply`.

To make it easy to update the version number automatically, instead of setting the `default` parameter of `var.version`, you can put the value into a *terraform.tfvars* file in the same directory as the Terraform configuration files. It uses the same HCL syntax as Terraform, so to specify values for your variables, you just provide a bunch of key-value pairs:

```
version = "ami-40d28157"
```

Whenever you run the `plan` or `apply` command, Terraform automatically looks for a *terraform.tfvars* file, and if it finds one, it uses any variables defined within it to set the variables in your configurations. The *.tfvars* file format is fairly easy to generate from an automated deployment script, although if you don't want to deal with HCL syntax, Terraform also allows you to use JSON in a *terraform.tfvars.json* file:

```
{
  "version": "ami-40d28157"
}
```

You can set up commit hooks to run your automated deployment script after every commit to the master branch of an application's repository. For example, the commit hook could deploy the app to staging if the commit message contains the text `"release-stage"` and to production if it contains the text `"release-prod"`. That way, deployments are triggered by commits and the history of all of those deployments ends up in your commit log. If something breaks in production, the commit log may be the first thing you check, as it now contains the information for both what code changed and what code was deployed.

Some Types of Terraform Changes Lead to Conflicts

What happens to this workflow if multiple team members are making changes at the same time? In Chapter 3, you saw that you can use a locking mechanism such as Terragrunt or Terraform Pro/Enterprise to ensure that if two team members are running `terraform apply` at the same time on the same set of Terraform configurations, their changes do not overwrite each other. Unfortunately, this only solves part of the problem. While Terragrunt and Terraform Pro/Enterprise provide locking for Terraform state, they cannot help you with locking at the level of the Terraform configurations themselves.

For example, let's say one of your team members, Anna, makes some changes to the Terraform configurations for an app called "foo" that consists of a single EC2 Instance:

```
resource "aws_instance" "foo" {
    ami           = "ami-40d28157"
    instance_type = "t2.micro"
}
```

The app is getting a lot of traffic, so Anna decides to change the `instance_type` from `t2.micro` to `t2.medium`:

```
resource "aws_instance" "foo" {
    ami           = "ami-40d28157"
    instance_type = "t2.medium"
}
```

Here's what Anna sees when she runs `terraform plan`:

```
> terraform plan

aws_instance.foo: Refreshing state... (ID: i-6a7c545b)
(...)

~ aws_instance.foo
    instance_type: "t2.micro" => "t2.medium"

Plan: 0 to add, 1 to change, 0 to destroy.
```

Those changes look good, so she runs `terraform apply` to deploy to staging.

In the meantime, Bill comes along and also starts making changes to the Terraform configurations for the same app. All Bill wants to do is to add a tag to the app:

```
resource "aws_instance" "foo" {
    ami           = "ami-40d28157"
    instance_type = "t2.micro"

    tags {
      Name = "foo"
    }
}
```

Note that Anna's changes are already deployed in staging, but as they have not been merged into master yet, Bill's code still has the old t2.micro instance_type. Here's what Bill sees when he runs the plan command:

```
> terraform plan

aws_instance.foo: Refreshing state... (ID: i-6a7c545b)
(...)

~ aws_instance.foo
    instance_type: "t2.medium" => "t2.micro"
    tags.%:        "0" => "1"
    tags.Name:     "" => "foo"

Plan: 0 to add, 1 to change, 0 to destroy.
```

Uh oh, he's about to undo Anna's instance_type change! If Anna is still testing in staging, she'll be very confused when the server suddenly redeploys and starts behaving differently.

The good news is that if Bill diligently runs the plan command and scans its output, he will realize something is wrong, and won't cause any problems for Anna. Moreover, such a problem could never occur in production, since this workflow requires all changes to be merged to master before they can be applied to the production environment.

Nevertheless, the point of the example is to highlight what happens when developers deploy changes to a shared environment before committing those changes to version control. You might be tempted to change the workflow to require submitting a pull request and merging to master *before* deploying to staging, but that approach has its own problems:

1. You now have no way to test your changes (other than the plan command) before submitting a code review. That means you'll be merging untested code into master, only to uncover bugs when you try to deploy that code to staging, so then you'll have to submit the fix for another code review, which is also untested, which means you'll be merging untested code into master...

2. Even if Anna's changes had been merged into master before Bill started working, but Bill simply forgot to update his local copy of the source code, the exact same problem would've happened anyway.

Let's take a step back and consider the typical process for updating code that is not infrastructure as code. For example, if you were updating a Ruby on Rails app, you would:

1. Make changes to your local copy of the code.

2. Test those changes locally, both through manual testing (running the Rails app on localhost) and automated testing (running the app's unit tests).

3. If everything works well locally, submit a pull request.

4. Once that pull request is merged, deploy your changes to staging.

5. If everything works well in staging, deploy your changes to prod.

The crucial difference between this workflow and the one outlined for Terraform is that with "normal" (noninfrastructure) code, you have the ability to test your changes locally before you submit a pull request and deploy them into a shared environment like staging. Since most Terraform code defines how to deploy infrastructure in a cloud environment, you can't test most Terraform changes "locally." That leaves you with two options:

Deal with conflicts

Use staging as a shared testing environment for all your developers and deal with conflicts as they happen. The conflicts will be relatively rare (until your teams get large), will only affect staging, and, as long as your developers are aware of the possibility of conflict and are diligent about running the plan command, most conflicts will be caught before they cause any problems.

More environments

If you have a large team that is making lots of Terraform changes and running into frequent conflicts in the staging environment, then you could create multiple staging environments instead of just one. With fewer developers in each environment, the chances of a conflict are lower. In fact, the gold standard is to allow a developer to spin up their own personal testing environment on demand whenever they are making infrastructure changes, and to tear those environments down when they are done. If all of your infrastructure is defined as code, this entire process can be automated. This is as close to doing "local testing" as you can get with infrastructure code, and it reduces the chances of a conflict to nearly zero.

If you go with the more environments option, you may find that managing a large number of environments by hand can become tedious and error prone. Once you're at this stage, you may want to start using a deployment pipeline.

Larger Teams May Need to Use a Development Pipeline

Let's say that you've decided that every member of your team (Ann, Bill, Cindy, etc.) can spin up an isolated environment for their own testing whenever they need it. Moreover, your company has expanded internationally, and now your code is deployed across AWS data centers around the world, including us-east-1, us-west-1, eu-west-1, and so on. You may end up with a folder structure that looks like Figure 6-2.

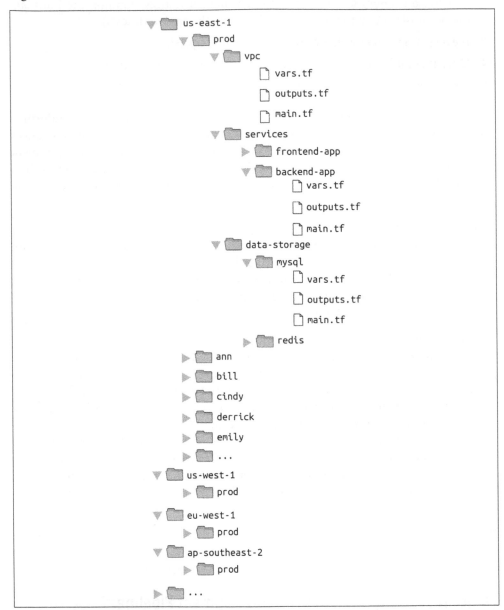

Figure 6-2. File layout with a large number of environments across many developers and many regions

Even if you are using Terraform modules, if each of those environments has a full copy of your entire stack—the VPC, the services, the data stores, and so on—you will still end up with a lot of copy/pasted Terraform code. This will make maintenance difficult and lead to errors where you make an update in one environment (e.g., us-east-1/prod) but forget to make the same update in other environments (e.g., us-west-1/prod).

One way to solve this problem is to use a *deployment pipeline*.[4] The general idea is to define the Terraform code in a single place and to create a pipeline that allows you to promote a single, immutable version of that definition through each of your environments.

Here's one way to implement this idea: in your *modules* repository, define all of your Terraform code for a single environment just as if you were defining it in the live repo (see Figure 6-3).

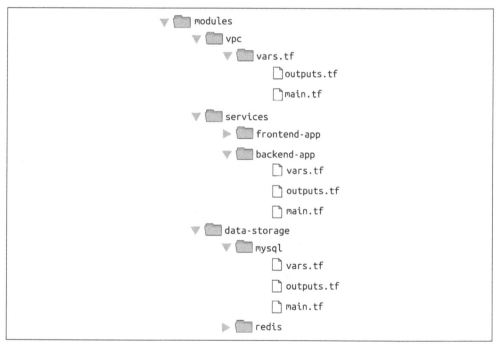

Figure 6-3. Define all the Terraform code for a single environment in the modules repo

Each of the components in the *modules* repo (e.g., vpc, frontend-app, mysql) contains standard Terraform code, ready to be deployed with a call to terraform apply,

---

4 Credit for this idea goes to Kief Morris: Using Pipelines to Manage Environments with Infrastructure as Code (*http://bit.ly/2lJmus8*).

except for one thing: anything that needs to vary between environments is exposed as an input variable. For example, the frontend-app module may expose the following variables:

```
variable "aws_region" {
  description = "The AWS region to deploy into (e.g. us-east-1)"
}

variable "environment_name" {
  description = "The name of the environment (e.g. stage, prod)"
}

variable "frontend_app_instance_type" {
  description = "The instance type to run (e.g. t2.micro)"
}

variable "frontend_app_instance_count" {
  description = "The number of instances to run"
}
```

In your live repository, you can deploy each component by creating a *.tfvars* file that sets those input variables to the appropriate values for each environment. Your folder structure in the live repo would look something like Figure 6-4.

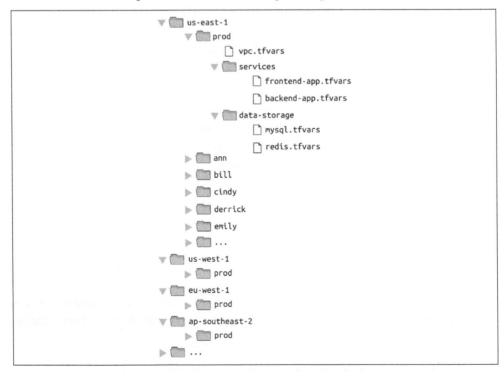

Figure 6-4. The file layout of the live repo when used with a deployment pipeline

Notice how there are no Terraform configurations (*.tf files) in the live repo. Instead, each .tfvars file specifies where its Terraform configurations live using a special parameter. For example, to deploy the frontend-app module in the production environment, you might have the following settings in *us-east-1/prod/frontend-app.tfvars*:

```
source = "git::git@github.com:foo/modules.git//frontend-app?ref=v0.0.3"

aws_region = "us-east-1"
environment_name = "prod"
frontend_app_instance_type = "m4.large"
frontend_app_instance_count = 10
```

To deploy a different version of the frontend-app module in staging, you could have the following settings in *us-east-1/stage/frontend-app.tfvars*:

```
source = "git::git@github.com:foo/modules.git//frontend-app?ref=v0.0.7"

aws_region = "us-east-1"
environment_name = "stage"
frontend_app_instance_type = "t2.micro"
frontend_app_instance_count = 2
```

Both .tfvars files specify the location of their Terraform configurations using the source parameter, which can specify either a local file path or a versioned Git URL. The .tfvars files also define values for every variable in those Terraform configurations.

To do a deployment, you can create a script that takes the path to a .tfvars file as an input and does the following:[5]

1. Run `terraform init` to check out the *modules* repo from the URL specified in the source parameter of the .tfvars file.

2. Run `terraform apply -var-file <TF_VARS_PATH>`, where TF_VARS_PATH is the path to the .tfvars file.

You could run this script to promote a single version of each component through each environment. For example, if Ann just released v0.0.7 of the frontend-app module, she could update the source URL to this new version in *us-east-1/ann/frontend-app.tfvars* and run the script to deploy the new version into her isolated testing environment. If the deployment succeeded and all the automated and manual tests passed, Ann could use the script to deploy the exact same version of frontend-app into the staging environment. Once again, if all tests passed, Ann could use the script one more time to promote v0.0.7 to the production environment(s). Of course, if the automated testing is thorough enough, Ann could even configure a

---

5 Terragrunt has support built-in for this workflow (*https://github.com/gruntwork-io/terragrunt*).

build server (e.g., Jenkins or Circle CI) to do all the promotions automatically so long as the automated tests were passing.

The benefit of this approach is that the code it takes to define an environment is reduced to just a handful of *.tfvars* files, each of which specifies solely the variables that are different for each environment. This is about as DRY as you can get, which helps reduce the maintenance overhead and copy/paste errors of maintaining multiple environments. As a result, developers will find it easier to spin up an isolated environment for testing, and tear those environments back down when they are done. Moreover, the pipeline idea allows you to treat your infrastructure code as an immutable artifact that you promote through each environment, as shown in Figure 6-5.

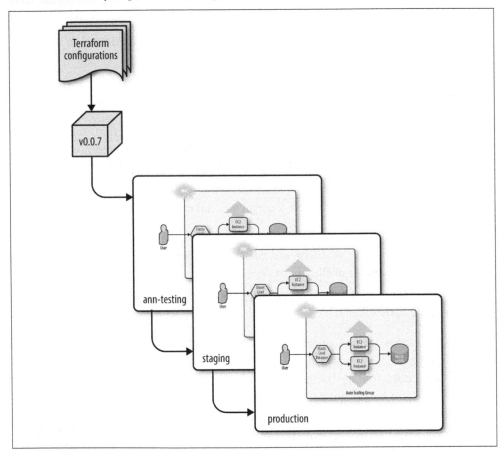

Figure 6-5. Promoting a specific version of the Terraform code from environment to environment

In Chapter 1, you saw how you can package an application as a versioned, immutable artifact (e.g., a VM image), and how that made it easier to test your application and ensure that it ran the exact same way in all environments. And now here, in the final chapter of the book, you are seeing how to package your entire infrastructure as a versioned, immutable artifact, and how that makes it easier to test your infrastructure and ensure that it runs the exact same way in all environments.

Conclusion

If you've made it to this point in the book, you now know just about everything you need to use Terraform in the real world, including how to write Terraform code, how to manage Terraform state, how to create reusable modules with Terraform, how to do loops, if-statements, and deployments, and how to use Terraform as a team. You've worked through examples of deploying and managing servers, clusters of servers, load balancers, databases, auto scaling schedules, CloudWatch alarms, IAM users, reusable modules, zero-downtime deployment, automated tests, and more. Phew! Just don't forget to run `terraform destroy` in each module when you're all done!

The power of Terraform, and more generally, infrastructure as code, is that you can manage all the operational concerns around an application using the same coding principles as the application itself. This allows you to apply the full power of software engineering to your infrastructure, including modules, code reviews, version control, and automated testing.

If you use Terraform correctly, your team will be able to deploy faster and respond to changes more quickly. Hopefully, deployments will become routine and boring—and in the world of operations, boring is a very good thing. And if you really do your job right, rather than spending all your time managing infrastructure by hand, your team will be able to spend more and more time improving that infrastructure, allowing you to go even faster.

This is the end of the book, but just the beginning of your journey with Terraform. To learn more about Terraform, infrastructure as code, and DevOps, head over to Appendix A for a list of recommended reading. And if you've got feedback or questions, I'd love to hear from you at *jim@ybrikman.com*. Thank you for reading!

Recommended Reading

The following are some of the best resources I've found on DevOps and infrastructure as code, including books, blog posts, newsletters, and talks.

Books

- *Infrastructure as Code: Managing Servers in the Cloud* by Kief Morris (O'Reilly)
- *Site Reliability Engineering: How Google Runs Production Systems* by Betsy Beyer, Chris Jones, Jennifer Petoff, and Niall Richard Murphy (O'Reilly)
- *The DevOps Handbook: How To Create World-Class Agility, Reliability, & Security in Technology Organizations* by Gene Kim, Jez Humble, Patrick Debois, and John Willis (IT Revolution Press)
- *Continuous Delivery: Reliable Software Releases through Build, Test, and Deployment Automation* by Jez Humble and David Farley (Addison-Wesley Professional)
- *Release It! Design and Deploy Production-Ready Software* by Michael T. Nygard (The Pragmatic Bookshelf)
- *Leading the Transformation: Applying Agile and DevOps Principles at Scale* by Gary Gruver and Tommy Mouser (IT Revolution Press)
- *Visible Ops Handbook* by by Kevin Behr, Gene Kim, and George Spafford (Information Technology Process Institute)
- *Effective DevOps* by Jennifer Davis and Katherine Daniels (O'Reilly)
- *Lean Enterprise* by Jez Humble, Joanne Molesky, Barry O'Reilly (O'Reilly)

- *Hello, Startup: A Programmer's Guide to Building Products, Technologies, and Teams* by Yevgeniy Brikman (O'Reilly)

Blogs

- High Scalability (*http://highscalability.com/*)
- Code as Craft (*https://codeascraft.com/*)
- dev2ops (*http://dev2ops.org/*)
- AWS blog (*https://aws.amazon.com/blogs/aws/*)
- Kitchen Soap (*http://www.kitchensoap.com/*)
- Paul Hammant's blog (*http://paulhammant.com/*)
- Martin Fowler's blog (*http://martinfowler.com/bliki/*)
- Gruntwork blog (*https://blog.gruntwork.io/*)
- Yevgeniy Brikman blog (*http://www.ybrikman.com/writing/*)

Talks

- "Adopting Continuous Delivery" (*https://youtu.be/ZLBhVEo1OG4*) by Jez Humble
- "Continuously Deploying Culture" (*https://vimeo.com/51310058*) by Michael Rembetsy and Patrick McDonnell
- "10+ Deploys Per Day: Dev and Ops Cooperation at Flickr" (*https://youtu.be/LdOe18KhtT4*) by John Allspaw and Paul Hammond
- "Why Google Stores Billions of Lines of Code in a Single Repository" (*https://youtu.be/W71BTkUbdqE*) by Rachel Potvin
- "The Language of the System" (*https://youtu.be/ROor6_NGIWU*) by Rich Hickey
- "Don't Build a Distributed Monolith" (*https://youtu.be/-czp0Y4Z36Y*) by Ben Christensen
- "Real Software Engineering" (*https://youtu.be/NP9AIUT9nos*) by Glenn Vanderburg
- "Infrastructure as code: running microservices on AWS using Docker, Terraform, and ECS" (*http://www.ybrikman.com/writing/2016/03/31/infrastructure-as-code-microservices-aws-docker-terraform-ecs/*) by Yevgeniy Brikman

- "Agility Requires Safety" (*http://www.ybrikman.com/writing/2016/02/14/agility-requires-safety/*) by Yevgeniy Brikman

Newsletters

- DevOps Weekly (*http://www.devopsweekly.com/*)
- DevOpsLinks (*http://devopslinks.com/*)
- Gruntwork Newsletter (*http://www.gruntwork.io/newsletter/*)
- Terraform: Up & Running Newsletter (*http://www.terraformupandrunning.com/#newsletter*)

Online Forums

- Terraform Google Group (*https://groups.google.com/forum/#!forum/terraform-tool*)
- DevOps subreddit (*https://www.reddit.com/r/devops/*)

Index

Symbols

"${ }" interpolation syntax, 41
* (splat character), 111
? : (ternary syntax), 115

A

ad hoc scripts (in IAC), 4
agent versus agentless software, 23
Amazon DynamoDB, 66
    using in Terragrunt to acquire and release locks, 68
Amazon machine image (AMI), 35
    creating with Packer, 10
    deploying new AMI across web server cluster, 123-134
    finding ID using aws_ami data source, 150
    ID of, in version input variable, 159
Amazon Resource Name (ARN), 65
    providing ARNs of IAM users as output variable, 111
Amazon S3 (Simple Storage Service) (see S3)
Amazon Web Services (AWS)
    and portability between cloud providers, 17
    fetching read-only information from, using data sources, 73
    Free Tier, 29
    IAM user environment variables, 33
    reasons for using to learn Terraform, 29
    regions, 34
    Relational Database Service (RDS), 73
    setting up your AWS account, 30
Ansible
    comparison to other IAC tools, 17-28
    executing code across web servers, 6
    playbook, defining and executing, 7
    role configuring a web server, 5
API calls to providers, 15
asynchronous APIs, 141
attributes of resources, looking up, 41
authentication options, 34
auto scaling group (ASG), 49
    autoscaling_group_name parameter, 94
    instances of, 54
    resizing and self-healing, 57
    updating min_size and max_size parameters to input variables, 92
    viewing in the console, 55
    zero-downtime deployment using create_before_destroy, 125, 136
auto scaling schedules, 93
    creating for some module users and not others, 113
availability zones, 34, 51
    deploying one EC2 Instance per zone, 135
AWS (see Amazon Web Services)
aws_ami data source, 150
aws_autoscaling_group resource, 54, 127
aws_autoscaling_schedule resources, 94
    defining in a module and conditionally creating for some users, 113
    increasing servers in cluster at a set time, 136
    setting autoscaling_group_name parameter, 95
aws_cloudwatch_metric_alarm resources, 116
aws_db_instance resource, 75
aws_elb resource, 127
aws_iam_policy resource, 112

setting count value returned by a conditional, 115
using to simulate loops, 108-113
count.index, 109
using with element and length functions, 110
CPU credits alarm, 116
CPU utilization alarm, 116
create_before_destroy parameter, 50
for zero-downtime deployment of ASGs, 126, 136
using carefully, 140
curl tool, 44, 57, 80, 133

D

data sources, 51
aws_ami data source, 150
fetching read-only information from AWS, 73
using terraform_remote_state to fetch read-only state, 73, 76
databases
Relational Database Service (RDS), 73
updating terraform_remote_state data source for, 91
db.t2.micro instance class, 75
declarative languages versus procedural languages, 19, 107
default parameter (variables), 46
dependencies
complicated, testing, 147
create_before_destroy parameter settings and, 127
implicit dependency in AWS, 42
resource dependencies and file layout, 73
deployment pipeline, 163-169
description parameter (variables), 46, 155
desired_capacity parameter, 57
of ASGs, 136
developers, operational skills and, x
DevOps, ix
core values, culture, automation, measurement, and sharing (CAMS), 3
goal of, 2
recommended reading on, 171-173
rise of, 1
diff output, reviewing for code, 158
DigitalOcean, 15, 29
(see also cloud providers)

distribution of code, configuration management tools, 6
Django, 40
DNS
DNS name of Elastic Load Balancer, 55
DNS name of ELB, exposing in a module, 95
Docker, 2, 7, 19
purpose of, 11
documentation, 154
code, 155
example code, 155
with IAC, 14
written, 155
Domain Specific Language (DSL), 153
Don't Repeat Yourself (DRY) principle, 45
DOT (graph description language), 43
DSL (Domain Specific Language), 153
dynamic data, inability to use in count parameter, 134
DynamoDB (see Amazon DynamoDB)

E

EC2 instances (see instances)
editors, writing Terraform code in, 34
Elastic Load Balancers (ELBs), 29, 52, 57
DNS name, exposing in a module, 95
element function, 110, 122, 135
encryption
in S3 storage of Terraform state, 64
support by Amazon S3, 62
environment variables, 46, 75
IAM user, 33
PATH, 33
environments
defining in separate sets of configurations, 69
deploying configurations into isolated test environment, 148
separate folders for, 70
staging and production, 83
using different version of modules in, 99
using multiple staging environments, 163
eventual consistency, 141
externalized files, 80

F

files
and file paths in modules, 96
externalized, 80

loops, 108-113

M

main.tf file, 63, 71, 74
maintenance, agent software and, 24
MAJOR.MINOR.PATCH format (semantic versioning), 102
map input variable (example), 47
master versus masterless server, 22
math in interpolations, 119
maturity, comparison for IAC tools, 27
meta-parameters, 50
mgmt folder, 70
modules (Terraform), reusable infrastructure with, 86-105
    file layout for modules, 156
    module basics, 88-90
        syntax for using a module, 89
    module gotchas, 96-98
        file paths, 96
        inline blocks, 96
    module inputs, 90-93
    module outputs, 94
    module versioning, 99-104
        in development, 104
    repository for modules, 144
modules folder, 100
MySQL database, 74
    providing address and port to web server cluster, 76
    Terraform files for, 74

N

name parameter, changing for resources, 139
name tag, adding to aws_instance, 37
names, hard-coded, module reuse and, 89
networks
    isolation of, 99
    network topology defined in VPC, 69
numbers, corecion to strings in Terraform, 47

O

OpenStack, 15
    (see also cloud providers)
OpenStack Heat, 12
    comparison to other IAC tools, 17-28
operations, x
    treating all aspects as software, 3

output variables
    accessing on terraform_remote_state data source, 77
    defining, 48
    exporting aws_security_group IDs as, 98
    for modules, 94
        accessing, syntax for, 94
    printing Amazon resource name of S3 bucket, 65
    returning ARN of an IAM user as, 111
outputs.tf file, 71, 74

P

Packer, 7, 19, 35
    purpose of, 11
    server template (example), 10
parameters, immutability of, 140
password managers, using, 75
password parameter (var.db_password), 75
path.module, 96
policies (IAM), 112
port numbers, root privileges and, 40
prevent_destroy parameter, 64
private subnets (VPC), 45
procedural languages versus declarative languages, 19, 107
prod folder, 70
production environment, 83
    avoiding duplication between staging environment and, 85
    deploying code to, 159
    running in same VPC as staging environment, 99
    setting new input variables for modules, 91
    using a module in, 89
providers, 34
    (see also cloud providers)
    removing provider definition from module main.tf file, 88
    updating provider parameter to aws_region input variable, 151
provisioning tools, 12
    (see also server provisioning tools)
    configuration management tools versus, 18
public subnets (VPC), 45
Puppet, 2, 5
    comparison to other IAC tools, 17-28

About the Author

Yevgeniy (Jim) Brikman loves programming, writing, speaking, traveling, and lifting heavy things. He is the cofounder of Gruntwork, a company that provides DevOps as a Service. He's also the author of another book published by O'Reilly Media called *Hello, Startup: A Programmer's Guide to Building Products, Technologies, and Teams.* Previously, he worked as a software engineer at LinkedIn, TripAdvisor, Cisco Systems, and Thomson Financial and got his BS and Masters at Cornell University. For more info, check out *ybrikman.com.*

Colophon

The animal on the cover of *Terraform: Up and Running* is the flying dragon lizard (*Draco volans*), a small reptile so named for its ability to glide using winglike flaps of skin known as patagia. The patagia are brightly colored and allow the animal to glide for up to eight meters. The flying dragon lizard is commonly found in many Southeast Asian countries, including Indonesia, Vietnam, Thailand, the Philippines, and Singapore.

Flying dragon lizards feed on insects and can grow to over 20 centimeters in length. They live primarily in forested regions, gliding from tree to tree to find prey and avoid predators. Females descend from the trees only to lay their eggs in hidden holes in the ground. The males are highly territorial and will chase rivals from tree to tree.

Although once thought to be poisonous, the flying dragon lizard are of no danger to humans and are sometimes kept as pets. They are not currently threatened or endangered.

Many of the animals on O'Reilly covers are endangered; all of them are important to the world. To learn more about how you can help, go to *animals.oreilly.com.*

The cover image is from *Johnson's Natural History.* The cover fonts are URW Typewriter and Guardian Sans. The text font is Adobe Minion Pro; the heading font is Adobe Myriad Condensed; and the code font is Dalton Maag's Ubuntu Mono.

Learn from experts.
Find the answers you need.

Sign up for a **10-day free trial** to get **unlimited access** to all of the content on Safari, including Learning Paths, interactive tutorials, and curated playlists that draw from thousands of ebooks and training videos on a wide range of topics, including data, design, DevOps, management, business—and much more.

Start your free trial at:
oreilly.com/safari

(No credit card required.)

Lightning Source UK Ltd.
Milton Keynes UK
UKHW030810260119
336176UK00003B/8/P